WHY I W ITE POETRY

WHY I WRITE POETRY

Essays on Becoming a Poet, Keeping Going and Advice for the Writing Life

Edited by Ian Humphreys

Nine
Arches
Press

Why I Write Poetry

**Essays on Becoming a Poet, Keeping Going
and Advice for the Writing Life**

Edited by Ian Humphreys

ISBN: 978-1-913437-29-9
eISBN: 978-1-913437-30-5

First published November 2021 by:

Nine Arches Press
Unit 14, Sir Frank Whittle Business Centre,
Great Central Way, Rugby.
CV21 3XH
United Kingdom

www.ninearchespress.com

Printed in the United Kingdom by:
Imprint Digital

Nine Arches Press is supported using public funding by Arts Council England.

Supported using public funding by
**ARTS COUNCIL
ENGLAND**

Also available from Nine Arches Press

52: Write a Poem a Week. Start Now. Keep Going
Jo Bell

How to be a Poet: A 21st Century Guide to Writing Well
Jo Bell and Jane Commane

The Craft: A Guide to Making Poetry Happen in the 21st Century
Edited by Rishi Dastidar

Contents

IAN HUMPHREYS

Why I Write Poetry: Essays on Becoming a Poet, Keeping Going and Advice for the Writing Life – An Introduction

The poets (by which I mean all artists) are finally the only people who know the truth about us. Soldiers don't. Statesmen don't. Priests don't. Union leaders don't. Only poets.
– James Baldwin

This book is an unravelling. Two dozen contemporary poets were tasked with trying to unpick the whys and wherefores of what they do. It could have been messy. But instead, clarity emerged from chaos.

Why poetry? How did they begin? What inspires their art? How did they find their voice? Who are their influences? How do they cope with set-backs and deal with success? What keeps them writing? Has the road been straight or long, winding and pot-holed? The answers are eye-opening, honest and compelling; clear-cut and implied. No two essays are alike. Yet many speak to each other, openly or subtly, in the same way that good poems communicate with one another.

Why I Write Poetry is a luminous display of frankness, intellect and wit from a cross-section of today's British poetry scene. These are writers who matter. Poets with many collections under their belts sit alongside newer voices, and contributors originate from all corners of the UK and beyond. Some have collections with big publishers, others are championed by small independents. Some write in English as a second language or use dialect, others stride across genres. Perhaps without realising it, many are dismantling the barriers between page and stage.

Despite representing a wide range of backgrounds, our essayists have one thing in common – a desire to write towards their own particular truth. This might centre on family, the environment, place, community, trauma, the body or politics. It may involve a dissection of the body politic. Collectively, these are must-read reflections of society's hopes and fears, our prejudices and dreams. Many of the essays include tips and advice on making your way in the competitive, often perplexing world of poetry, and there's a wealth of thought-provoking prompts and exercises to enjoy.

Audre Lorde said, *only one thing is more frightening than speaking your truth. And that's not speaking.* By rooting out the truth and beauty of why they write, our featured poets underscore not only why poetry matters to them, but why it should matter to everyone.

Thank you to the thinkers who contributed their time and energy to this project. There were surprises and delights at every turn. Thanks also to Jane Commane for the gig, for her continued support, and for coming up with the concept and title of this vital, timely book.

*

The late poet John Ash once pleaded with me not to take up poetry.

It was 1983. He had cornered me in the newly renovated kitchen of a house in Whalley Range. John rented the adjacent room. My friend Tarik rented a room on the second floor. Another friend Mark was pirouetting by the dishwasher when John stormed in to complain about the noise.

We had been giddily fixing 3am snacks while attempting an off-key rendition of 'Love Pains' by Yvonne Elliman, so it was a fair cop. John didn't stay angry for long. He asked what I was studying, what my plans were, and seemed relieved to hear they did not involve poetry.

'Good choice, very sensible. Whatever you do, please don't become a poet! Stick to something where you can earn a bit of money.'

I remember laughing to myself. At that moment, I honestly could not think of anything I would enjoy less – an occupation that seemed duller – than writing poetry.

While researching this book, I discovered that around the time we met, John had written a short essay about his collection *The Goodbyes* (Carcanet, 1982). The piece was republished two decades later in *Don't Ask Me What I Mean: Poets in Their Own Words* (Picador).

One part of the essay, in particular, caught my eye: "… many of the poems were written to the accompaniment of the kind of music you might hear at parties or in good nightclubs, that is to say, songs of August Darnell, Ashford and Simpson or the Chic Organisation, and on occasion the words of these songs have found their way into the poems."

If only John had mentioned this during his pep talk. Perhaps I wouldn't have waited 30 years before starting to write poetry myself. At school, we were taught the Romantics, nothing modern. After sitting my A-levels, I did not pick up a book of poems for two decades. I was unaware that contemporary poetry celebrated popular culture, that a 'serious' lyric poet could be inspired by August Darnell aka 'Kid Creole' of Kid Creole and the Coconuts.

John and I hardly spoke again. Once, over burning toast, he recommended Prince's overlooked early albums. A year or so later, I heard he had moved to New York where he became associated with the New York School of poets.

Several poems in my debut collection *Zebra* (Nine Arches Press, 2019) explore my coming of age in 1980s Manchester. The gay club I had frequented the night John advised against poetry as a vocation is a touchstone in the book. I began to write about those early days on and around Canal Street, I think, to try and work out something about my formative years. For sure, there was joy, exhilaration and freedom. But there was also fear; a background dread that we accepted back then as part of life's rhythm, as relentless as the four-on-the-floor beat of those Hi-NRG hits we lived for. It was fear of the unknown. Fear of illness. Fear of society's disapproval which at any moment could mutate into danger.

Such contradictory emotions can be difficult to articulate, as slippery as a lager-soaked dancefloor. What I longed to communicate was feeling not fact, and this seemed best conveyed through the shimmering medium of poetry.

The need to voice the unsayable – reach for the ungraspable – is one of the main reasons I write poetry. It's a motive I share with many of my peers. When I turned to social media to ask why poets do what they do, many replied with answers along the lines of:

> *To make sense of life.*
> *To make sense of the world.*
> *To connect with my inner world.*
> *To say things I could not otherwise express.*

Another response that came up, again and again, was *compulsion*:

> *I write poetry because I must.*
> *It is a thing I do, like breathing.*
> *I wrote poetry before I could write.*
> *I can't help myself.*

Over one hundred poets responded, with variations on these two themes accounting for around ninety percent of all answers put forward. This posed a question: how could we prevent our contributors from writing multiple versions of the same essay?

The answer? Jane and I identified what we most admired in the work of the selected poets. We then asked each of them to explore a theme reflecting this idiosyncratic quality as they riffed on their craft.

As you will discover, the tactic worked wonders. The resulting twenty-five essays are fascinating and varied. There's little repetition, and thankfully even less navel-gazing.

Each piece is unique in its approach to the trials, tribulations and pleasures of writing poetry. The mix of styles is satisfyingly rich, from the informal to the academic, the lyric to the dreamlike. Together, the compositions stand as testament to the robust state of poetry in 21st century Britain.

Had I not started writing eight years ago, I would have missed out on so much, including the chance to curate and edit this book. As such, I am delighted I listened to instinct rather than advice, and eventually shimmied my way towards a calling, of sorts, in poetry.

ROMALYN ANTE

Pusikit: On Working as a Poet whilst Working for a Living

Can I tell you a secret? In 2010, when I was applying for British residency five years after my mother brought the whole family to the UK, I confused 'middle name' with 'middle initial'. In the Philippines, it's customary to write the first letter of our mother's maiden name between our given name and surname. So, across the petal-bright paper of the official form, I scribbled my mother's maiden name: *Pusikit*.

When I think of this blunder now, I am reminded of poet Richard Blanco's words in 'My Father in English': "the exile who / tried to master the language he chose to master him". Despite living in England for many years now, I still cannot seem to tame the language of the country that has so much control over me and other migrants like my family. When I started writing poetry in the midst of April snow in 2012, the same year I graduated as a nurse, people made comments about me and my writing: "You will never be a poet here in the UK, your grammar is just bad." Worse, some people also assumed that not being able to talk like them meant I understood less. Someone even asked me once, "Do you really get what this book means?"

However, there is a memory, a place, that goes beyond people's discouragement. When I think why I write, I am sucked back to my childhood years when my family could not afford a tricycle fare to send me to school. To reach the school where I could learn English, I waded through the intense heat, my cheeks stinging in the sun, my backpack indenting its weight into my shoulders. I also got soaked in the sharp rain of June, the sole of my worn-out shoe slapping the wet asphalt like a dead person's tongue.

When I was about eleven, my playmate-neighbours joined their nurse-mother in Canada. My siblings and I clambered over their steel gates to rummage through the left-behind boxes of books. Those thrown-away things were treasures for us: books with damp bindings, pages with corners embroidered in yellow-green mould. But the letters, the words, were still ebony-stark, as if they were printed yesterday. I did not grow up in a house tinged with the smell of old books but whenever the moon rose from behind the dark-blue misted peak of Suso ng Dalaga in the distance, my maternal grandfather, Tatay Lolo, would gather me and my siblings to recount myths and folk tales. We would gape at his gesticulations as candlelight flickered across his wrist and hand. Through his voice, I grew to love language, its music, and the sweet perfume of the evening breeze suffusing his words.

The truth is, in our village, Tatay Lolo's surname *Pusikit* equated to only one thing: poor people. His mother died in childbirth when he was eight. By the season of rambutan, his father brought a new woman into their home and turned to his five half-orphaned children and said, "You must stop going to school now, since you've already learnt how to count." If you know how to count, you can work the menial jobs without getting duped. So at such a young age, Tatay Lolo became a kargador in the market, fetching basins of water from the river for the fishmongers, scrubbing gut-stenched stalls at the end of the day. Sometimes, he would sleep on a butcher's table, staring at the Milky Way's diagonal blur in the sky before closing his eyes.

The Pusikit were notorious for coming from angkan ng mga mahihirap or the clan of the poor. But Tatay Lolo never stopped working. At thirteen, he started sweeping the floor of our town's barber shop. He swept and swept until a panel of sunrise on the black marble swelled into the buzzing of customers, extending to the raucous cries of vendors from across the street. He swept and swept until the owner clicked the door locked.

A barber offered him a job in Manila, where he was taught how to trim hair and blade the edges of the back clean. At night, Tatay Lolo climbed into the attic of the barber's shop, where he was given a bed (a mattress, really), but he would scramble down again to lie on the green plastic bench next to the scissor rack because his mattress was infested with surot: biting ticks which left his arms and chest stinging in blisters. I imagine him lying on the bench (as he once did on the butcher's table), still gazing beyond what was above him, past the monsoon moths around the light bulb, until the shadows buried him in the rustling darkness.

When Tatay Lolo was eighteen he went back to our town, carrying nothing but a black pouch with two scissors and one plastic comb, to start his own venture. On the first day, he had one head to trim, on the third, it was doubled. He met my grandmother, Nanay Lola, who was working as a helper at a tiny boutique across the road from where he found a space for his barber's. The other vendors told Nanay Lola, "Don't go for that man, he's poorer than a rat." But young people's hearts, though naive, see deeply into things that the knowledgeable can be blind to.

They married and rented a space on the ground under someone's stilt house, living among the chickens and a stray dog. When Tatay Lolo's tally reached a hundred heads per day, they could afford a small room. Days and years passed like snippets of hair falling into dark drifts, and they managed to build a small hut they could at last call their own. But they were struck by fate again when their first son, Donald, fell ill. Their son was eight years old when he was diagnosed with a congenital heart disease. One morning at the hospital, Donald sat up in bed, called for his siblings, and turned to Tatay Lolo and said, "Tatay, magaling na ako." *Tatay, I'm healed.*

When his three siblings arrived – my mother, the youngest among them – he kissed each one on the cheek and turned to

Tatay Lolo again to ask, "Tatay, ako'y inyong buhatin." *Tatay, carry me in your arms.*

"Tatay, ako'y ididlip lang." *Tatay, I'm just going to take a nap.*

Tatay Lolo lulled him, feeling his son's head dangled over his right shoulder, his breaths gurgling at his neck, his little chest caving in, as if collapsing into his. Soon, the exhalations slowed until there were no more breaths. That year, the monsoon season was dimmer and trees pelted against Tatay Lolo's roof. Lightning flashed across the rafters and it sounded like Donald's laughter. One morning, Nanay Lola ran to Tatay Lolo to hand him a purple umbrella. "Go to the cemetery. Our son might get wet in the downpour."

"Darling, our son is dead." Tatay Lolo looked down at his feet.

When we were growing up, Tatay would gather us children on the terrace. Candle flickering at his wrists, Tatay would tell us that ghosts are real – for on the night of Uncle Donald's wake, he had seen him at the foot of his bed, gazing down at him in his burial shirt made of the cheapest pineapple fibres. A curtain billowed and he was gone. At that time, I understood only that kind of haunting.

French-Cuban American diarist and essayist Anaïs Nin said: "We write to taste life twice, in the moment and in retrospect." Perhaps this is true. But perhaps writing goes further than to serve the writer in private too. I'd like to think that when Tatay Lolo narrated his story, writing those words in the wind, he also invited us to *live* it, so, like him, we could make sense of it, learn from it, and, perhaps, acquire values from it. Be strengthened by it.

When my mother grew up, Tatay Lolo sent her to study nursing.

"You can't do it," his fellow barbers said. "You can't send your daughter to college. Nursing is a course only for the rich!" When Ma got pregnant during her second year of college, the barbers said, "Do not send her back to college since she has a husband now."

Still, Tatay Lolo snipped as much hair as he could, trimmed many sideburns clean.

"Why would you discourage someone who perseveres?" Tatay Lolo once asked, when I was on an international call to him. Though I knew the question was not just for me.

Whenever Tatay Lolo got home after working all day in the barber shop, I'd pull off his shoes and massage his feet to find little snippets of hair in between his toes, as if they were fine black needles jabbed into his skin. I'd massage his palms to feel the bumpy callouses from the scissor's grip.

Tonight, I am on a call to him again. The window shines with the amber glow of powdered snow. I have just qualified as a nurse, working in a renal dialysis unit. Like many Filipinos who grew up from *angkan ng mga mahihirap*, I've always promised myself that I would get a secure job so I can help my family in the future. This means only one thing: go into nursing. I wanted to do a writing course at the university, but I was too scared to borrow money from the bank, thinking that in the end I would only have a writing diploma and an empty pocket.

Today, I am telling Tatay Lolo about the patients I care for: those whose kidneys shrunk like Nanay Lola's. For a moment, we remember what Nanay Lola told him after she developed kidney failure, and our family's resources (Tatay Lolo's decades of savings) started to drain away: "Sell our wedding rings, sell this small house. Are you just going to let me die?"

I think of the young me, stepping onto an upturned, empty paint jug to take a look at Nanay Lola's swollen face under the coffin glass. I think of the summer when all the trees of our town seemed to convulse with the mockery of sparrows as we dug my grandmother out of her grave because we could no longer afford to rent the land she was buried in. Those dark flumes of hair still attached to her mud-crusted skull.

"Dialysis patients here are lucky, Tatay Lolo," my voice cracks through the line. "They get everything. Their treatment is free, their hospital food is free. Even the cotton I press onto their skin as I take the needle out is free."

"I'm happy you are over there now. Your mother has given you a good life, so live it," Tatay Lolo says.

When I write, I write of this. I write for people like us: the poor, the losers in this lottery. Those who cannot afford the ground for the final resting of their bones.

I write too to praise my mother in the winter of 2003 – a woman from the Philippines arriving alone in England as a staff nurse, in a second-hand green quilted coat.

I think of her working on a ward, dodging as many phone calls as she could, in case she did not understand the English accent, the Black Country twang on the other line. I can see her speaking to a young, pregnant fifteen-year old who corrected her English. The bushfire on Ma's face as her patient giggled at her word choices: not *period*, but *full stop*.

Yet the young mother learned from Ma too: when they both stared down at the bilirubin-glow of her urine in the pulp bowl, and Ma spoke of her condition, Rh incompatibility – how her own antibodies can attack the baby's blood cells. I think of the moment Ma's palm traversed the globe of her patient's abdomen, how both of them smiled when Ma felt a kick near the navel.

Ma learned to adopt the antibodies of a foreign land. She started saying *trousers*, not *pants*, *aubergine*, not *eggplant*.

When I started writing whilst working full-time as a nurse, I promised myself to persevere, just like my Tatay Lolo, just like Ma. Between breaks, I study poetry books, flicking through a dictionary from time to time. As I trudge through the bright corridors of the hospital, I listen to the echo of my own footsteps, attempt to pace them into iambic pentameter. As I auscultate a thin chest to listen for a heart murmur, I imagine the movement of a murmuration of starlings against the caramel sun. The little sounds created when I twist the key in the drug cupboard or pop another pill into a pot would move something in me, urge me to suddenly pull the handover notes from my pocket and scribble a line or two on the back of it. As I give an arm injection and my patient looks away, his nape strained and bright in the light, I would remember that moment, store it away, and later, when I write it down, it travels with me through my long working days, expands even into places I know I haven't been.

"Tatay Lolo, I've sent so many poems, but I keep getting rejected."

"Tatay Lolo, I won a competition, but someone says it is only because I write about nursing and because I'm pretty."

"Tatay Lolo, I have a book deal but I keep getting anonymous emails saying I don't deserve it."

Those are the words that travel only through long-distance calls. But now I know that I share these words as prayers not for reassurance, but for strength. Perhaps in the same way that Tatay Lolo's thoughts travelled beyond the expanse of the night sky as he lay on a butcher's table when he was young.

I still feel a touch of anxiety when I sit with a pen poised above the fragility of a page. Every time I look at my British passport, it reminds me of my embarrassing error, a mistake written in black and white: *Pusikit*. But I know why I write. I know for whom I write, and I know the place I'm writing from.

In *Letters to a Young Poet*, Rainer Maria Rilke writes: "Find out the reason that commands you to write; see whether it has spread its roots into the very depth of your heart; confess to yourself you would have to die if you were forbidden to write."

I write to tell our story – the story of the poorest and the losers. The ones who tried to crawl out of darkness until their fingers were calloused and bleeding. I write to tell the story of us and the people or patients we meet along the way. These are the lives I want to turn the spotlight on, because in that light they help me realise the true values and virtues of living. I write to live and relive pain and fear, and hopefully, in the process of this crafting, to somehow be transformed too.

Faced with the anxiety of officialdom, I once confused 'middle name' with 'middle initial', and now I bear my mother's maiden name, my grandfather's surname. Can I tell you another secret? Pusikit is not only the surname of the poor. It is also an old Tagalog word that means 'impenetrable darkness'. It was even used in some poetry I remember reading from a book left behind by our neighbour who migrated to Canada: "Sa gabing pusikit." *At the night of impenetrable darkness.*

I write because I must, even though sometimes the world (and I myself) doubts and mocks. Today, I received another rejection. Today, I received more anonymous hate mail, deriding the fact that my book is still not listed for a literary prize: "You can never be a poet here in the UK." I eat discouragement for breakfast. But the world does not know this: my clan was born out of darkness; I am not afraid to be unseen. We were nobodies; I am not afraid to have nothing.

The phone line crackles. Outside, the blizzard riots and the squall thunders above our roof like a passing Boeing. Tatay Lolo tells me, "When you're in that impenetrable darkness, only the brightest of lights can touch you."

Romalyn Pusikit Ante

 Writing Exercise

Look at the history of your name. Does it mean anything or has someone in your family (or in your village) attached a meaning to it? Perhaps you have a made-up meaning for your name? If your name bears a certain colour, what would it be?

Write about this.

MARY JEAN CHAN

Queering the Poem:
On Writing One's Intersectional Truths

What I love most about poetry is the way it carries the weight of everything: history, a mother's grief, queer shame, intergenerational trauma, fear, and even that heaviest and most difficult of emotions – joy. I remember reading Thomas Hardy's 'The Darkling Thrush' as a sixteen-year-old and coming across these lines: "The tangled bine-stems scored the sky / Like strings of broken lyres". His poem made me see the tree outside my childhood home in Hong Kong in a different light, as if I were looking out of a new window. Poets like T.S. Eliot, Matthew Arnold and Sylvia Plath spoke quietly to me, between the hectic schedule of school and competitive sports, or in dreams, which asked of me strange questions I had no answers for. I read Shakespeare's *Twelfth Night* and became infatuated with Viola/Cesario. I found myself wondering if I could dress like Cesario and fall in love with Viola.

Like my literary crush Viola/Cesario, I was a fencer. In 2006, I joined the Hong Kong SAR Fencing Team as an épéeist at a national competition in Shanghai. On the day of the competition, I found myself nursing a twisted left ankle injury, which was heavily taped. I could not move as well as I had hoped to and soon found myself sitting in the stands, having lost my round-robin bouts. I watched dejectedly as the others continued to compete. Suddenly, I heard footsteps and looked up to find my best friend on the team in tears. Sensing her anguish, I placed my arm around her and held her tight. We sat like that for a while. Then I felt a sharp pain on my left shoulder. It was my mum, who had flown to Shanghai to watch me compete. The look she gave us made me believe that my arm around my friend's shoulder was the closest I would ever get to love. *Let me*, my mum eventually said, filling the space between us.

*

For years, I kept that part of me silent. Silence can be a mode of survival. It was not until I arrived at Swarthmore College in the United States in 2009 that this previously unspoken facet of my life seemed suddenly fathomable. It was as if a small window had opened in my mind and I could see the sky again. In the spring of 2010, a friend told me about the poet Adrienne Rich. That afternoon, I went to the library and read Rich's poem 'Dedications'. I read it three times, then found myself whispering these words, over and over:

> I know you are reading this poem
> as the underground train loses momentum and before running up the stairs
> toward a new kind of love
> your life has never allowed.

I remember crying in bed that night, out of gratitude, relief and a hesitant joy. As I read more of Rich's work, I began – over the following weeks, months and years – to resolve to become an active participant in this thing called poetry: to become a writer, in addition to being a reader. For the first time in my life, it seemed possible. I began reading more widely, and discovered writers such as Audre Lorde, June Jordan, James Baldwin, Walt Whitman, Muriel Rukeyser, Emily Dickinson, Mary Oliver, Frank O'Hara, Langston Hughes and Nikki Giovanni, among others. Line by line, these poets changed my life. I remember committing these lines from Lorde's poem 'A Litany for Survival' to memory:

> but when we are silent
> we are still afraid
>
> So it is better to speak

Despite coming out to close friends in college, I struggled for years with the idea of coming out on the page. In my earliest poems, I remember trying to efface myself. By that I mean: I was trying to disappear. During my senior year in college, I remember sitting in my dorm room with an Asian American friend who was also an aspiring poet. I showed him a recent poem of mine and waited to hear what he thought of it. After a few minutes, he looked at me and said: "I love your work, but I can't seem to see you in it." His comment touched a nerve. What was I so intent on hiding, or disguising? What could I not bear to write down, in black, on the blank page? In her poem 'Cartographies of Silence', Rich writes: "Silence can be a plan / rigorously executed / the blueprint to a life / It is a presence / it has a history / a form".

*

What makes a poem queer? In her seminal book *Queer Phenomenology: Orientations, Objects, Others* (2006), Sara Ahmed contends that "race [is] a rather queer matter", when one considers how "whiteness is invisible and unmarked, as the absent centre against which [non-white] others appear only as deviants or as lines of deviation". As a queer Chinese poet, I am reminded of the truth of Ahmed's words during the Q & A after a poetry reading, when an audience member asks me to read a poem in Chinese. In that moment, my race becomes a queer matter. In a poem about sexuality, the speaker – the lyric I – is not raceless. In a poem about postcolonial grief, the speaker – the lyric I – remains queer. For solace and inspiration, I have recently turned to Chen Chen, an Asian American poet whose work encapsulates what I most admire in a queer poem. In his poem 'I Invite My Parents to a Dinner Party', Chen writes with equal parts humour, bitterness and courage about the gargantuan effort it often takes to queer the Chinese dining table's perennially straight lines:

> In the invitation, I include a picture of my boyfriend
> & write, *You've met him two times. But this time,*

you will ask him things other than can you pass the
whatever. You will ask him

about him. ...

The queer poem allows for intersectionality as a lived, embodied experience. In the 'Preface' to his debut poetry collection *This Wound Is a World* (2019), Billy-Ray Belcourt writes: "Poetry is creaturely. It resists categorical capture. It is a shape-shifting, defiant force in the world." A poem is queer if it asks complex questions about our own relationship to gender, sexuality, race, class, as well as history, culture, family and inheritance, and allows the poet to reconfigure their relationship with others as a social being. The queer poem is also future-oriented. In *Cruising Utopia: The Then and There of Queer Futurity*, José Esteban Muñoz writes: "We have never been queer, yet queerness exists for us as an ideality that can be distilled from the past and used to imagine a future." The queer poem, then, is hopeful by definition. It imagines what is not yet possible, but might one day become so. Sometimes, the queer poem is a wish which stems from desire. I have often read Rainer Maria Rilke's poem 'Lament' from *The Book of Hours* as queer, since it deals with rupture, loss and grief, but also expresses a fervent hope for change:

> I think there were tears
> in the car I heard pass
> and something terrible was said.
>
> .   .   .   .   .   .
>
> I would like to step out of my heart
> and go walking beneath the enormous sky.

*

In 2019, I published my debut poetry collection, *Flèche*. One poem contains this line, which has guided my life over the past few years: "One day, it becomes a choice: to walk out of this life, or to begin living mine" ('A Wild Patience Has Taken Me This Far'). The poem is wiser than I am; I am still trying to follow in its footsteps. Yet I do follow, tentatively, hesitantly. Many of my poems in *Flèche* are, in Sharon Old's words, "apparently personal". A few years ago, I came across the concept of 'lyric shame'. In her compelling book *Lyric Shame: The Lyric Subject of Contemporary American Poetry*, Gillian White discusses how this shame around the lyric poem first emerged out of the "anti-expressive", "anti-meditative" and "anti-epiphanic" agenda that took over the US academy in the 1990s. In defining lyric shame, White cites a self-conscious poem by Robert Hass called 'Interrupted Meditation', in which he states: "I'm a little ashamed that I want to end this poem / singing, but I want to end this poem singing".

The power inherent in the lyric 'I' makes me wonder: who gets to say 'I' without fear, without shame? In her ground-breaking poetry collection *Citizen: An American Lyric* (2014), Claudia Rankine observes the power dynamics that exist between a white speaker and their racialised counterpart: "…a world begins its furious erasure – / Who do you think you are, saying I to me?" I am aware of the lyric shame that many Black, Asian, mixed-race and ethnic minority poets face from writing into and out of their lives, in case it is read by inattentive critics as wholly autobiographical or as lacking in any aesthetical or imaginative qualities. Since my book's publication, I have grappled with the thought of veiling or complicating the lyric 'I' in my forthcoming poems, so my speakers cannot be easily linked to an essentialised queer, racial Other. However, having grown up in a socio-cultural environment in which having a false self was necessary for my survival, I firmly believe that to write freely from the perspective of the queer and racialised self is a radical act. It is up to critics and readers to understand that the poem – especially the queer poem – seeks nothing more (and nothing less) than to do justice to the beautiful and joyous complexity inherent in a human life.

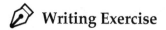 **Writing Exercise**

Picture in your mind's eye what Sara Ahmed calls "a kinship object", such as a dinner table around which a 'we' might gather. Write a poem that attempts to queer the straight lines of this kinship object.

What are the implicit rules that this 'we' adheres to? How might the speaker disrupt this?

Remember the importance of imagery (metaphor and simile) in conveying tensions and unspoken truths. Recall Emily Dickinson: "Tell all the truth but tell it slant".

ANDREW McMILLAN

The Body I Could Trust:
On Writing and the Changing Voice

My first forays into poetry, 'serious poetry' I'll call them, were angst-ridden scribblings when I was sixteen – trying to somehow imitate Thom Gunn (and yes, unkind critic, maybe you could say I'm still doing the same thing now).

We all write because we love reading, it's important to remember that, and to keep that balance tipped firmly towards input rather than output as our careers develop. As we shift and grow, we might keep trying on different voices, different formal styles, like a child let into a dressing-up box at school for the first time.

I often end up telling my students that the most interesting poets are the ones who read as widely as possible, all their different influences eventually being blended together in a voice that could only be theirs. The notion of a 'voice', as in what it is we write and what drives it to be written, needs constant nourishment, or it grows stale. I don't really want to write another Andrew McMillan poem again, or I want what an 'Andrew McMillan poem' is to be constantly shapeshifting.

After a while of sending things out to magazines, I put together a first pamphlet and found a publisher for it, Red Squirrel Press. It was called *Every Salt Advance* (because I hadn't yet landed on my affectation for one-word plosive titles) and it contained mainly first-person lyric poems about lost love, or the seemingly endless propensity towards unsuitable others that my body seemed charged with. It was received okay, but there was one review that I'll always remember (we always remember our bad reviews don't we; it's evolutionary I think), which said that it was too personal, too concerned with itself, and thus nobody would be interested. Because I was young and new I took that to heart. I think when we start out, after those first furtive years of writing in secret, we make the mistake of believing we're writing for an audience rather than for ourselves. So I shifted gear. I looked around at what was fashionable at the time and I put together a second pamphlet, *The Moon is a Supporting Player*, which, as you can probably tell from the title, was more experimental, was more playful and arch and ironic and everything that I'm never comfortable being but felt my poetry had to be. I was writing for that imagined audience rather than myself. If the first pamphlet had got a bit of notice, some positive and some negative, then this one sank without a trace. I think it's because it felt inauthentic, it felt like someone imitating the voice of someone else. A lot of poets can do irony and playfulness very well, but I've never been one of them.

After that second pamphlet, I kept reading as much as possible. I graduated from university, I moved back to Barnsley, I broke up with my first long-term boyfriend. Whilst all that was going on, I began to write little snippets of things, which were never really going to be full poems but which felt too important to throw away. Eventually, over a couple of years, these built into one long poem which explored the recession in Barnsley, Thom Gunn, and my own heartbreak. It felt in that poem that I was leaning back into what I'd written at first, lyric-driven, first-person quite personal poems. I'd tried on other voices and it didn't work, and so I went back to working on the voice that I had. I gave up imagining an audience; I just wrote the poems I felt I had to write at the time. The rest, I decided, could follow.

*

I can remember where I was when I began to draft the poem 'Urination', which is one of the poems from my debut collection *physical* which people tend to remember. I was in Shrewsbury, coming home from a reading I'd just given, juggling my workbag and overnight suitcase as I popped into the station toilets. I mention this only to speed up the inevitable installing of the blue plaque just above the urinal. 'Urination' is part of a small group of poems, 'the men are weeping in the gym', 'strongman', 'choke', etc., which really felt like, as they were coming, that I was finding the notes my debut collection wanted to play.

Whenever you publish a book, I think there are two different versions of it: there's the one that people assume it is and the one that it actually is. A cover, or the way a book is (hopefully) reviewed and discussed, can form people's impressions of the contents in a way which can be much more powerful than what those contents actually are. I think there was a general sense that perhaps my first book was quite sexy or erotic and there's really barely anything sexual in it (for a bit more of that you want book two); rather, I'd argue the real subject was the male body. It's not an original thought, but it had always struck me that the history of poetry was, generally, men looking at women (mostly without their permission) and writing poems of longing and yearning towards them. I suppose, retrospectively, I can say I had a simple mission: what if that male gaze was turned on other men – only partly in a homosexual way, but also in a homosocial way? The result of that is what you get in *physical.*

It perhaps seems strange for a poet to say, but my main influences as a poet are actually novelists. The main one is Jon McGregor. Jon is a master of the plain line, of speech without speech marks that still somehow feels like speech, of a distilled phraseology of prose that contains endless depths. He's responsible, perhaps more than anyone, for the style that I was pushing at and working on during *physical.* So I was going to hold the male gaze on the male body, and I was going to try and do that as plainly as possible.

Once that decision had been taken then it seemed to me that the job of the poet, or indeed any artist, was to commit to that entirely, to not look away. A poem about the body cannot be like a coy scene in a film where a couple are about to have sex and then the camera cuts away to a curtain flapping in the wind, and then cuts back to the happy couple having a cigarette afterwards. If the poem is to look at the body, then it has to look at the body entirely, in all its ugliness and awkwardness and imperfection. A poem of the body is not a hagiography of the self: it is a mirror in a harsh light, there can be no hiding of anything.

*

So after my first book came a second one, as is the natural way of things, and I remember floundering around for a long time trying to work out a direction for that second book. I somehow had in my head that it had to be something dramatically different, a wild change of direction that would surprise everyone. But just as I couldn't fake it with my second pamphlet a decade before, nor could I just suddenly fake a new change in direction for my poetry. My editor had some wise words, which I'll badly paraphrase here, that the work would change as I did, because I'd grow and change as everyone does, but I had my sensibility, my way of looking at the world. That was immensely reassuring, and I think quite empowering as well.

One of the things which seems to preoccupy a lot of poets when they first start out is a search for a 'thing', what is their great subject going to be, what's the unique topic that they're going to tackle? Of course, there's validity in that, but I do think that too often we can lose ourselves in theorising what that 'thing' is before we've gone out and lived it and discovered it by chance. So often our subconscious already knows what it wants to be fixated on, and our job is just to open the empty page onto which the ideas and thoughts can spill out. I didn't actively choose to be a poet of the body, or queer male desire, or masculinity, or any of the other labels that are often put onto my work. I simply wrote about a life I was living, a world I saw around me, bodies that I was encountering on a nightly basis.

And why write? It helps me make sense of things, it helps me, eventually, to move I think towards some sort of catharsis and redemption. Also, I think, in that great Sharon Olds sense, I write because I hope it might be useful. There's a perverse myth that people who write poetry that errs towards the confessional must be conceited or self-centred. I don't think this is true, beyond the normal amount that it's true for any artist. If I was a poet of nature, I'd show you a tree, not really because that particular tree is of special interest or value, but rather because maybe it can say something about the beauty of creation, or the solidity of the natural world. In the same way, I don't think anything that's ever happened to me is particularly interesting, nor do I particularly think anyone should care, but if I show you a body I encountered, if I show you a loss, if I show you my own body, then perhaps behind that glimpse is something bigger, something that could be said about desire, or love, or intimacy.

The thing is, ultimately an audience makes what it wants to of your work, if it makes anything at all. It's better to imagine one will never be read, and to take that as something very freeing. Write the work that you wish you'd had a chance to read when you were starting out.

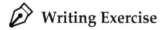 **Writing Exercise**

Think of something which has been preoccupying you lately. Something that comes to you at 2 a.m. when the neighbours' security light comes on, or that you turn over in your mind as you make your way to work on the bus. That thing that lodges itself inside of you. That thing you can't get rid of, but that you've not yet been able to write about.

Normally, I'd say, put that at the top of your blank page, try and write about it, but I think that automatically making something the 'subject' of your writing is not actually useful.

So: make a note of that thing at the BOTTOM of your page, and instead of writing ABOUT it, write TOWARDS it, in whatever way you take that to mean (chronologically, emotionally, geographically).

You might never get to the thing itself, you might find a divergent route on your way towards it where the real poem dwells, but write towards it, write into that vibration of uncertainty and trepidation. The poem is the journey, it's not the destination.

JEAN SPRACKLAND

In Praise of Emptiness:
On Writing about Place and Paying Attention

When I started out, I used to write poems on the backs of bills and shopping lists, though I could certainly have afforded to buy a notebook. I was enthralled by poetry's capacity to emerge and exist without requiring any equipment at all. Painters and sculptors, photographers and film-makers are obliged to acquire machines and materials, to house them, to learn how to use them, to lug them from place to place. Poetry on the other hand is absolutely portable, and can be completely immaterial. There's no studio, no darkroom, no kiln, and no case full of expensive lenses to maintain, clean, repair and generally fiddle around with when the creative work is in abeyance.

One of the effects of this is to throw the poet back on their own resources, to make them acutely conscious of starting from scratch, or not starting at all. It's hardly surprising if that leads to orgies of doubt and self-recrimination. Truth is, I expend a lot of energy on *not* writing poetry, and my faith in it has always felt flimsy and tenuous. Not in poetry itself – that's a different kind of faith, and I'll never stop *reading* poems – but in my capacity to go on writing them. Between poems – and especially between books – I go through long barren spells in which the prospect of writing another one seems remote, barely imaginable. I feel deskilled, incapacitated. It's as if the whole thing were a conjuring trick, and I've forgotten not only how to do it but what it's for.

So persistent is this phenomenon, and so common – poets angst about it all the time – that I've come to the conclusion it's not only inevitable but necessary. Rather than seeing it as a problem, which one day I must solve somehow, I've learnt to recognise that feeling of incapacity as an essential part of a recurring process. It plays a role in returning me to a crucial state: a state of *emptiness*. Some poets characterise their fallow periods as times when they have to wait for the reservoir to refill. But that metaphor doesn't work for me. In my case, it's not a question of filling, but of pulling out the plug and letting it drain to nothing. Only then can I start again.

It takes time, and I know of no shortcuts. But eventually, after days or weeks or months, there comes a moment when the intense preoccupations that drove the last poem, or the last book, have swirled away with the muddy water it left behind. All the thinking and questioning that went into that piece of work have gurgled down the plughole, and the accompanying noise and chatter are nothing more than the occasional residual drip. Then I become aware once more of a space, a silence, a latency. It occurs to me that something new may be possible after all.

In other respects, too, I have long understood emptiness to be a creative necessity. I'm drawn to places that look empty. A windswept beach where the sea is a grey line in the distance, for example. I tramped up and down that beach hundreds of times thinking "there's nothing here", before becoming attuned to its distinctive character, its moods and cycles and fluctuations. It was as if I hadn't really been looking at all. Then that flat, grey landscape sprang into three dimensions and became a place of teeming possibility. Other places have a different kind of emptiness – they're like vessels that have not been filled with thoughts and theories and writing and art. Perhaps these places are not usually given the status of *place*. Perhaps they are disqualified because they don't meet the usual aesthetic standards. They tend to be overlooked or undervalued, seen as too small, too ordinary or too familiar to be worth writing about at all. These are exciting spaces for the poet to move into and explore, relatively free of literary antecedent. And of course, there is no such thing as an uninteresting place; every street corner and motorway service station, every path and pond and playing field is a place of radiant potential, once we're paying attention.

Attention is the key, of course. It's the sine qua non of the poet. Whatever other resources we bring to writing – facility with language, understanding of form, distinctiveness of voice, and so on – it's the quality of attention that matters first and foremost. Every poet starts out as a watcher, a listener, an obsessive observer of the world around them, stashing things away in the subconscious for later. They learn to build on that natural curiosity, training themselves to look, and keep looking, long after others have transferred their gaze to other things. (It's why the adjective 'unflinching' is such a trope of the poetry book jacket blurb.) Elizabeth Bishop described it as "perfectly useless concentration", marking it out as different from the more functional kind of attention we pay when crossing the road or following a recipe.

That phrase "perfectly useless concentration" reminds me of the kind of looking you had to do to make sense of those 'magic eye' pictures that were all the rage in the nineties. Each one started out as a page of repeating shapes, apparently random in pattern – overlapping tiles, scales or leaves – and you'd have to gaze at it very intently, sometimes for several minutes, before the hidden picture emerged. Success depended on a convergence of two things: distance, and intensity of concentration. The concentration had a particular double quality to it: the intensity was combined with a kind of permissiveness. You had to maintain a laser-beam focus, while simultaneously relaxing, letting go, allowing that change of perception.

With practice, the eye and the brain developed a knack. You might have to either lean in closer, or stand back a little; finding the right distance was often the trick that would suddenly pop the image into another dimension, and there it was: dinosaur, solar system, shoal of tropical fish. Once you'd seen it, it was peculiarly hard to unsee it.

The poet's attention is not solely visual, so the likeness is not a literal one. But there are some parallels. When I'm writing about something – a place, an object, a person – I want my attention to spring it into an extra dimension. I want to perceive it differently, to make out another truth beyond or within the obvious. That means concentrating very hard, while letting go at the same time; and it means moving closer, or further away, experimenting with distance. And each of these two imperatives intensifies the other; in the words of Gaston Bachelard, "attention is by itself an enlarging glass".

This is the only way I can make any sense of the absurd and pompous idea that poets are visionaries: a hyper-Romantic notion, trailing its gauzy fantasies of special callings and supernatural gifts. Transferred from the poet to the poem, however, it's a different matter. The making of a poem as a visionary activity: yes, that feels both true and important. There are revelations, perceptual shifts, moments of synthesis which become available to us when we write, and part of what makes this happen is our way of looking. We can train ourselves to see differently, to make out forms and meanings that are not apparent to that more functional, everyday kind of looking we do when we prepare to step off the pavement or weigh out sugar and flour.

Many years ago, on a writers' and artists' retreat, I struck up a friendship with a ceramicist who was working on a series of etched tiles, and went out with her into the nearby forest to watch her gather material for her work. I followed a few steps behind as she walked in silence along the forest paths, stopping every now and then in response to some prompt I had neither seen, heard nor felt: a tapping of one branch against another, perhaps, or a few drops of rain darkening the sandy earth. She opened her sketchbook, fixed the branch or the patch of earth with an intense, immovable gaze, and began to draw. I was amazed to see that she was drawing *without looking at the page at all.* After a time, she shut the book and walked on.

Such a simple practice, but so illuminating to watch. I went out on my own later that day and began to experiment. I remember that on that walk I came across the remains of a car, burnt out and abandoned long ago. I looked hard at what was left: a rectangle marked out in black, scattered with snakes of molten metal, a sheaf of copper wires, pieces of mirror mottled with orange, parts of a printed circuit. I flipped open my notebook and wrote without looking at the page. I still have it, torn from the book and kept as a reminder of that walk, that way of looking. Of course it was wonky, and one of the sentences ran off the edge of the paper into thin air. Only some of it is legible, but the indecipherable parts are just as important: ellipses, lacunae, inviting and alive with potential. When I look at that pencil scrawl I experience again the thrill of that moment, the sense that I'd hit on something. It seems too simple to call a method, and it isn't methodical. But it is a practice, a way of encountering places and the stuff we find in them.

I tore out the page and kept it, but the notebook is lost. Not thrown away, but lost in the jumble of notebooks, some stuffed into a huge drawer (which thanks to the weight of them has fatally slipped its runners), others in a removal crate in the loft. I am an ardent scribbler in notebooks, but a terrible keeper of them. It would undoubtedly be better to be more organised, but I just can't. Then again, a bad habit nurtured and sustained over a lifetime must be serving some kind of purpose. This one is surely linked to the intuition that my writing emerges from chaos and anarchy, that disorientation and 'lostness' are ingredients in the creative mix, and that having noticed the burnt-out car and jotted some semi-legible notes is enough for now. I'm not going to rush home and write that poem.

I might write it a year or two later, when I drag out the impossibly heavy drawer to excavate its contents, as I do from time to time, and pull at random from the heap of notebooks that particular notebook. It will be an accidental find. I have a good memory for places and what happened in them, so I'll recall that in a clearing half a mile further on I found one of the car seats, its nylon cover slashed with a blade, and its green lap full of acorns. And that I was at that moment literally lost, and was thinking of the seat and the burnt remains as landmarks by which to navigate my way out of the forest. But time will have put some distance between those scribbled notes and their original source, and the memory will have softened and loosened, been mythologised a little. It's true that the making of a poem begins long before we write down the words; but writing itself is a way of paying attention, and of working out what's there. The notes both belong and do not belong to the moment they tried to capture. They achieve a measure of freedom, and are now the makings of something new.

So I think of writing not as an activity, but a state. A state of attention, a state of spatial and temporal distance, and above all a state of emptiness. My task is to find my way into that state. When I do, I feel about poems, as John Ashbery did, that "they're going on all the time in my head and I occasionally snip off a length".

Why bother? There's no money in it, and no one is hammering on my door demanding the next instalment. There's plenty not to like: the anxiety, the self-doubt, the dead ends and the ink wasted. It's simply that when I am able to find a way in, it's uniquely absorbing, and I never feel more real than when I'm absorbed like that.

✏ Writing Exercise

In the moment I found the car seat in the forest, the world was turned inside out. Something that belongs in a closed and quasi-domestic space had been torn from its fixings, carried some distance and left exposed to the elements. It was fashioned to support the human body, but there was no one here but birds and squirrels. It looked naked, injured and bereft. There was something shocking about it that made me want to look away, and at the same time compelled me to look.

Imagine an indoor object taken outdoors, or an outdoor object brought indoors. How does it look, feel or smell? What is happening to it in its new environment – how is it affected by weather, or by central heating? Is it visited by anyone, human or otherwise? Or has it been entirely forgotten? What memories or dreams are held in its materials? And what future awaits it now?

W. N. HERBERT

What Is thi langwij a thi guhtr Using Us For? On Poetry and Dialect

What is it that you're doing if, like increasing numbers of non-RP (received pronunciation) poets from William Letford to Liz Berry, you write something in your 'local' voice? In my case it would be the Dundonian dialect of the Scots language – and I must confess, as soon as I've said that, I feel a temptation to sidestep my own question and start arguing instead about what is meant by local, by dialect, by language. That would of course be to trap my foot in my very own mouth.

Consider the question put to the novelist Val McDermid in the wake of the 2021 Scottish elections by Sky News reporter Adam Boulton: "...would you like to see an independent Scotland abandon speaking the sort of English we're speaking now?" When Val replies first in English then in Scots, there is a moment of stunned silence, before he completely misses her point about functional bilingualism.

That point is it's not a matter of either/or. We can do both – or if we stick at Gaelic on the old Duolingo, all three. The first great joy of having another way of speaking is the simple fact of plenitude, of being rich in words. But when the use of our 'other' speech carries, as here, political significance, and when, as here, the power balance is in favour of a monoculture, how quickly joy is subverted into defensiveness.

Let's acknowledge, for argument's sake, that argumentativeness plays some small part. Does it describe fully the motivation of the poet who writes in Scots or another English? No. Why would you want to do that, assuming you aren't in it for the pie fight, unless there was something expressed in that plenitude which was worth the strangeness-to-others with its potential drop in reader numbers – something, moreover, which was inherently what poetry is all about?

We understand that such affiliations to the local are made under the shadow of the centre, and are therefore partly a resistance to its arguments about universality. That would be one sense in which Tom Leonard wrote in Glaswegian, or Linton Kwesi Johnson writes in Jamaican. So, by using non-standard English, you are always making an implicit statement about locality over centrality, or at least suggesting: *here is a centre too*.

In discussing the work of Tom Leonard, the poet Theresa Muñoz says: "Leonard's work ... articulates the painful space between individuals and whatever they are alienated from; be it an absence of belonging to a community, or within their own minds and bodies as they struggle to understand their own identity. ... Linguistically, formally, in social and historical contexts, Leonard's exploration and commitment to this theme is a continuous presence in his writing."

Many of us have been informed, through looks, shrugs, and half-heard comments, or bright, explanatory corrections, that there's something wrong with the way we speak. The worst part of this is when we do it to ourselves, as individuals, family members, or neighbours, as workmates and teachers and bosses: subdividing ourselves against ourselves, across and within social divides, across and within families, out from and deep within the self.

We eagerly join our 'superiors' in pitting accent against accent, background against background, religion against religion, seizing on race, gender, sexual orientation, using class as a fissiparous, vicious, constantly splintering weapon we keep picking up by the blade and not the handle.

'You' can never be like 'us' in this rigged game in which 'we' have to substitute authenticity for property, but then, as we secretly realise, 'we' have never really been like ourselves either.

Using Scots, using dialect, is our counter-argument. It says: "You, O Standard English, may be understood pretty much anywhere – and certainly are by us – but there are many like us, all experiencing the unfairness of this word game, and all our localities are stitched together by this realisation, so we are comprehensible not just to our near neighbours, but, through the principle of localised, individual expression, to all such minorities everywhere, and are approachable by them on that principle."

So let's oppose the tendency to tendentiousness with a mode the users of alternatives to English often avail themselves of: not taking ourselves (too) seriously. The deadpan and deeply surreal Scottish comedian Chic Murray performed a parody of a Scots poem which captures this (transcribed here from a recording):

> Ae day when the ecks and slaggets dog
> and loo that fleg when ickets beg
> O greg and slag when of its doo
> will rise and waw the grigget.
>
> O gravet grun when ickets beg
> and loo the seg when ickets tek
> O gravet nicket icket bag and aye!
> and slew the fleggan neck ...

He's halfway through the next line when the audience's howls of laughter make him pause, mock-affronted. He tries to resume, but claims to have lost his place while (apparently) impersonating an owl:

> Ae day when lags and lickets end
> and waw the pu o hogget – HOO!
> oh whit was that? OHOO! OHOO! –
> ah lickets dae when ickets deck – OHOO! –

He races anxiously through the whole thing again, thus emphasising both its almost complete lack of sense and its entirely coherent structure.

Thinking about how this idea of incomprehensibility is symbolised by the Lallans-heavy Scottish poem – indeed how perfectly that marries two assumed obscurities: that of the language with that of poetry itself – I'm reminded of the strange contiguity of Chic's family home, on Bank Street, Greenock, to 1 Hope Street, the (almost optimistic) birthplace of W. S. Graham, key poet of the limitations of language.

This closeness of the closies almost embodies G. Gregory Smith's famous definition of the Caledonian Antiszyzygy: "the absolute propriety of a gargoyle's grinning at the elbow of a kneeling saint". And Chic's marvellous play on a poem, tongue-twisting Scots and nonsense, is as knowing as Graham's own dismissal of the "plastic" Scots of his day – he claimed to have overheard an argument among Hugh MacDiarmid's followers that the word "telephone" should be replaced with "farspeak".

Both are, satirically, part of the internal debate over how Scots are Scots allowed to be. In response to that debate, it seems to me that we gain two things through expressing ourselves in oor ain tongues, whatever they may be.

Firstly we access intimacy, a closeness that you feel not only to your centre but to the language that approaches it – there must be an aspect of the familial, of the language of lovers, in that relation between words and place. This is the intimacy won in Liz Berry's 'Oh Sweethearts':

> We'm side-by-side on the grass,
> me barefeet in the water,
> bowing our heads, gentle
> as osses at the water trough.

This intimacy is not limited to speakers of said tongue: every year, without knowing what half the words mean, millions of revellers greet the New Year with 'Auld Lang Syne' precisely because that closeness survives. As Micawber puts it in *David Copperfield*, "'I am not exactly aware … what gowans may be, but I have no doubt that Copperfield and myself would frequently have taken a pull at them, if it had been feasible.'"

Secondly, as Micawber intimates, we experience a bracing strangeness in the very fibre of intimacy, because it is being rendered strange to you by that overarching standard. This means you must be awake to use your own language, keenly aware of its procedures in order to access the gowans or other minute particulars by its use.

Your centre, then, is always ec-centric, and the 'real' centre of things is rendered, by this awareness, an ex-centre, clinging to a power over your imagination it has – nearly – lost. And because this centre has been made strange unto you, by age or experience, education or migration, economics or social pressure, you use this language in the hope it will allow you to go home.

Hame may be right before you but slightly displaced, or in the past, even somewhat idealised, but you're used to being told such desires are nostalgic, sentimental, whimsical, inauthentic, unrealistic, limiting, or even coorse. In fact, you've long been aware that there seems to be a special vocabulary for belittling the sort of thing you do, as though that were, somehow, part of the exercising of power that maintains the standard.

This phenomenon is one the United Kingdom has long been in denial about, perhaps because it undermines simplistic notions as to what that unity means. It is diglossia, the situation where there are two versions of the same language, one theoretically 'high' status, and the other supposedly 'low', but both acknowledged as co-existing, as in what was defined in Greek as *Katharévousa* and *Dimotikí*. People codeswitch between the two according to social context.

In Britain, the singular status of the Home Counties/metropolitan understanding of RP has meant our other Englishes, and indeed other languages, are associated with class or race but denied even 'demotic' status. They are dismissed as ways of self-declaring your inferiority or imperfect grasp of a supposedly neutral, 'proper' speech.

This association with class compresses nations into cities or regions – so Scotland is made to fit into the Gorbals. Even more significantly, it locates these inferior non-languages in the spoken and not the written – it denies them literacy.

What Scots – a language withoot an army or a navy, but with a centuries-old literature – demonstrates is that there can be more than one 'high' language, even if the smaller has largely deferred to the larger, even if it has become (as arguably it does in the works of Hugh MacDiarmid) a sort of historical fiction about itself. Fundamentally, the class division does not fully describe our linguistic situation. Poetry in these other Englishes, therefore, is one way the working and middle classes of these islands reclaim their modes of speech as legitimate, ready to be transformed into writing.

It is in this diglossic sense that Val McDermid perfectly understands Adam Boulton, but Adam Boulton is reluctant to understand Val McDermid. It is in this sense that while anyone knows what is being satirised in Chic Murray's parody, his audience gets why he's doing it.

In 'The Beast in the Space', W. S. Graham describes the space between writer, poem and reader as a fraught territory crossed by something like meaning – I say "something like" because the beast seems not entirely identifiable with the meaning of the poem:

The beast that lives on silence takes
Its bite out of either side.
It pads and sniffs between us. Now
It comes and laps my meaning up.

It seems possible that Graham conceived of this frightening creature in its unknowable zone because he came from industrial working-class Greenock and went to high cultural Edinburgh and London, before retreating to bohemian penniless Cornwall. Being between language worlds is one way of understanding what Graham means by questions like "What is the language using us for?"

There are three stages to engaging with this understanding of Englishes, which take us from an unconsidered usage of 'dialect' to a meaningful awareness of how strange all this is. The first must be estrangement itself, where the words we've always used become as odd to us as we perceive them being to others.

It is in this sense that Hugh MacDiarmid combed the Scots dictionary, looking for terms that seemed at once deeply familiar and strikingly strange:

> We have been enormously struck by the resemblance ...
> between Jamieson's *Etymological Dictionary of the Scottish
> Language* and James Joyce's *Ulysses*. ... There are words
> and phrases in the Vernacular which thrill me with a sense
> of having been produced as a result of mental processes
> entirely different from my own and much more powerful.

The second is usage as an act of resistance to the perceived order, carried beyond the point of excess to break the mould. It is in this sense that Tom Leonard dropped MacDiarmid's strange words in favour of confrontational phonetic spelling:

> its thi lang-
> wij a thi
> guhtr thaht ...

The third is what happens when the mould is broken and what is uncovered is experienced as truth. Talking about the Greek word Αλήθεια in *A Primer for Forgetting*, Lewis Hyde puts it like this:

> How odd that the Greek word now translated as 'truth' is a *negative* – *a-lethe*, the *not*-forgotten, the *un*-concealed – the implication being that the ground condition of the world (or of the mind) is obscurity and mystery and that persons who speak the truth have done the work of (or been given a gift for) un-hiding, calling to mind what is otherwise veiled, covered, dark, silent.

This "un-hiding" may well be momentary – corresponding to the duration of a poem or book or grouping of writers, before being ossified into new dogma. For me it's summed up by this image from William Letford of coming home and hearing a street musician:

> I'd like tae tell um thit this is it ...
> ... standin oan a corner in yur hame
> toon, an audience eh one radge eatin a
> macaroni pie, bit singin, wee man, yur singin.

That moment seems to correspond to a famous scene in *Gregory's Girl* where the headmaster (played naturally by Chic Murray) sits at the school piano and rattles out a little tune, oblivious to the world around him. When the world, in the form of a couple of pupils, notices him, he pauses, declares, "Off you go, small boys," then carries on playing.

The tune is, apparently, Chic's own. The moment demarks a certain angle to things, both to who we appear to be and to how we relate to the world, which is, arguably, that won by the users of other Englishes: it is serene, independent, self-aware – and splendidly daft.

Writing Exercise

I often find that the most effective creative exercises are those I devise when working with kids. The element of play they involve seems to appeal to that part of us which still uses play to create.

When visiting my old school in Broughty Ferry as a 'Scots Language Ambassador', I would put word grids on the whiteboard to encourage discussion about the distinction between family words, 'local' speech, words regarded as slang, loan words, and words thought of as 'proper' Scots. These sorts of minute particulars are both extremely localised and generational, so words I'd use were no longer current, and words these teenagers would deploy were barely in my recognition vocabulary.

I think we found many of these terms challenging to bring to mind and to use in our writing as opposed to speech – there's an ingrained barrier against articulating words we know, but also know not to be 'proper'. So we'd use these categories to construct a 'class vocabulary' we all felt comfortable using. And that is what I suggest you do: build a vocabulary of twenty words you might draw on to play a couple of word games. Here's my grid:

Family words	Local words	Scots words	Other words
Pike – to peek or 'keek' as if from behind curtains	Peh – pie (normally understood as a Scotch or macaroni pie)	Pech – to pant, but also an old form of 'Pecht' or 'Pict'	Plenitude – in Scots this might be a 'routh'
Flech – to scratch as though a dog with fleas	Teck – something excellent, seemingly from 'technical'	Blether – to chat or gossip	Behemoth – a biblical creature (Job 40:18)
Mask – to brew tea	Ashet – a plate (loan word from French)	Fash – to be concerned, as in 'Dinna fash' (don't worry)	Plastic – currently undergoing an alteration of meaning from something adaptable and synthetic to something dangerously indestructible
Gussie – a segment of orange	Pus – face but with the charge of a swear word	Gowan – a daisy	Platypus – the creature which, when analysed according to categories of Enlightenment thinking, challenged those categories
Caa – to rock gently, as in 'caain awa' or 'just getting by'	Cundie – drain in a gutter (another loan word, from the French 'conduit')	Unca – unusual or distinctive (linked to 'uncanny')	Komboloi – Greek 'worry beads', derived from prayer beads, but not used for prayer

The first thing such grids throw up is provisionality – there could easily be other categories and words, and a different selection might be put together tomorrow or next week. Revisit your choices regularly – construct alphabets, phrase books, as you see fit.

How do your words relate to each other, within and across categories? I've picked a lot of mine because of how they rhyme and/or alliterate with each other – and they pun. This translingual punning is one of the unnoticed elements of working with dialects. So 'platypus' relates to 'pus', but it also echoes another Dundee word, 'pletty' – the platforms which ran along the outsides of some tenements. This seeing and hearing of words in other words is part of the enhanced experience of having Englishes, rather than an English.

So, what to do with your twenty words? Well, play. See how they fit together or don't in a single or several poems. Try using one a line – perhaps moving from family to other, or just as they suggest themselves. Cast out one word and bring in another if it suits better. Do any of your words rhyme, or do they suggest rhymes with other words? Are there any words you wouldn't dare use? Dare to use them.

This is like a cross between piano practice and doodling. You have to be prepared to say and scribble nonsense, and to throw a lot of it away. But every now and then, you enter into a new relationship with a word you may have used all your life, and that relationship sheds new light on that life. That is why we use our ain tongue, whatever it micht be.

LEO BOIX

Un Enfoque Latinx:
On Writing in Two Languages

In which language and in what register to write? The richness of Latin American and Latinx poetry comes from the many cultures, languages, dialects and backgrounds that has shaped it throughout the years. As a British Latinx poet, I have been formed by this complex multilingual and multicultural experience, which defines many aspects of my practice. Spanish is the language I was born into. It was, until I moved to the UK in 1997, the language of everyday life, of the books of poetry and fiction I'd read at school, the language of home and heart. When I arrived in England I couldn't speak a word of English. To describe this as frustrating would be an understatement. I tried language classes, but mostly learnt by reading books to myself, by listening to the radio, and by watching television in my tiny bedsit in Brixton.

I soon enrolled at Birkbeck College, where I studied Latin American literature and poetry, in English, while working part-time as an arts and culture journalist, in Spanish, for the main newspaper catering to the Latin American diaspora in London. This was a growing community of Spanish-speaking migrants from Latin American countries ravaged by decades of war, state violence and poverty. We were from Colombia, El Salvador, Chile, Nicaragua, Argentina, Bolivia, Mexico, Peru and Ecuador. I would share the newsroom with fellow Latin Americans, with whom I spoke mainly in Spanish, although I would often conduct my interviews in English.

This interviewing process proved informative to me as I immediately realised that the better I understood and expressed myself in English, the better the answers from my interviewees. I have since worked for many major newspapers and radio stations in Latin America, and also in the US, including for the *Miami Herald* (in Spanish). And throughout that time, I continued writing poetry in Spanish, publishing two books in Argentina.

*

Writing Spanish poetry in London increasingly led to gatherings with Latin American friends in cafés or homes to read our work. We founded a collective called Spanish and Latin American Writers and Poets (SLAP). This group was the first self-identified place to explore ideas of migration, diaspora, language barriers and exclusion, and it was through performing our work in various venues that I came into contact with activist and writer Nathalie Teitler, who became my mentor. Encouraged by her, I took a leap of faith and began writing poetry in English. This move was predated by much reading of poetry in English, from medieval to contemporary authors. That started to give me a sense of historical contexts and registers and also it was great way to gain vocabulary and experiment with words.

*

English is now the language I inhabit in my writing after so many years in this country, although I still read and write poetry in Spanish—though with less frequency. In recent years, my focus has shifted not only to English but also to a hybrid Spanglish. I have fully embraced bilingualism. Running poetry courses for bilingual students (at secondary schools with 70% of pupils first- or second-generation Latin Americans) has helped me appreciate that bilingual learning is a reality for many. I have also realised the importance of accepting non-anglophone cultures into the spectrum of diversity in poetry, not only voices from the Commonwealth – with its historical links to the UK – but beyond too. I have become aware that much decolonising revolves around the legacy of empire and commonwealth but cultures that were never part of the British empire have still suffered from the uneven distribution of power and its abuses and are a present fact of life in the UK. These groups tend to get further ignored because of language and cultural barriers.

*

Writing poetry in English, despite English not being my mother tongue, and the act (and meaning of the act) of writing a poem that contains words from several languages is a complex and multi-layered process, not to mention a laborious one. It often involves trying to distance myself from the English language, and moulding it outside of myself, as if I were sculpting an object, chipping away, carving it, as a gradually malleable thing, seen taking shape from a certain distance. Writing in Spanish on the other hand, comes easier, more immediately and more spontaneously, but at a price in that the labour of giving shape and form to the work is missing from this process. It is oddly harder for me to see my writing in Spanish than in English, because the process of writing in English is more fraught, more involved and more laborious. In any case, it is no coincidence that in English – a language that is *outside* of myself, yet very present – I am much more inclined to experiment with meaning, form, structure and syntax, whereas in Spanish I tend to instinctively listen for known sounds, music, rhyme, and repeatedly capture the everyday commonplaces from my youth in Argentina.

*

Living between the East End of London and the seaside town of Deal in Kent has meant that the language and stories I hear and experience appear with increasing regularity in my poetry. Often this is combined with or influenced by old English words or phrases that are juxtaposed with equivalents from my mother tongue. This finds its mirror also in terms of the visual imagery and experiences that appear in my work, from an imaginary and emotive Latin American landscape to the concrete (literally and metaphorically) streets of London or the coastal scenery of Kent. My words in English are increasingly connected to the lived experience here, to its specific locality, and new linguistic landscapes that arise with it. This sense of language as something that can and has been broken down and remoulded has inspired me to experiment with old English words and their associated ancient English folk tales. I take pleasure in seeing the English language in its various earlier stages of formation, watching it evolve much like the way my understanding of the English language evolves as I bring Spanish into closer contact with it. I often bring in different Latin American registers and stories, explore the idea of 'mistranslations' from classical English texts, and immerse myself in cultural translations, bringing Latin American poets to life in English.

*

The results of this linguistic process have caused antagonism, not only within myself in accepting the often messy experiment, but for other people, particularly those for whom a second language is entirely outside their reality. I remember going to poetry workshops where some participants would aggressively challenge my use of Spanish words while writing poetry in English. I was asked rather angrily during a seminar, "Why would you use *venteveo* if there is a word in English for *blackbird*?" Well, the answer is that *venteveo* conjures for me the bird that I'd often see in our back garden in Buenos Aires. It speaks of those specific memories related to my previous life in a subtropical suburb, whereas *blackbird* is for me an English bird.

This lack of acceptance of languages other than English is a phenomenon associated with a lack of experience with languages other than English. It is the logical outcome of expecting the rest of the world to accommodate the English language as the international lingua franca and one that stems ultimately from a sense of insecurity due to educational and cultural Anglocentrism. Much of the rest of the world would be able to incorporate English into its poetry if it wished, but so far, not the other way around. In parallel, I have experienced Spanish-speaking colleagues in the UK challenging me for "degrading" a Spanish word in order to create a new Spanglish term, and therefore "lowering the beauty of high Spanish". I have also been criticised for writing in English altogether, being occasionally told in casual conversation: "You shouldn't write poetry in another language that is not your mother tongue. Poetry is the language of the heart, and it ought to come naturally and familiarly."

*

Where possible I try to explore these areas of conflict in my teaching and mentoring. Through poetry workshop exercises I encourage participants to incorporate words from languages other than just English, to mix or use languages they don't know, to read poetry in translation, to guess the meaning of words by the way they sound or look on the page, to use words that they believe to be of foreign origin, and thus to explore the multilingualism inherent in any language. The reaction from some participants is of reticence, of fear of the unknown, and also rejection of anything that is not English, but often much fun is had in realising just how many words in current phraseology come from other languages or cultures. It is important to accept that there is a diversity of languages within the British experience – and that this is not to the detriment of the English language, but, on the contrary, enriches the poetry scene.

*

Language is an unruly thing: it rebels and moulds. Since living in the UK, language has become for me a soft, elastic and ever-changing thing. It is an evolving system that has adapted with me (and in me) as I've crossed continents, moved from culture to culture, from language to language. The tradition of the bilingual writer, moving between different sign systems and audiences to create a text in two languages or a 'mixed' language, is more than a personal and niche experience. It is an allegory for how a language changes over time, and therefore it is of value to everyone.

Within Latinx poetry there is a long tradition of poets using Quechua, Aymara, Mapudungun or Nahuatl mixed with Spanish, and also English in the case of Latinx writers working inside the anglophone world. One could argue that Latinx writers have always deliberately crossed boundaries between languages, reinvigorating Spanish in the process, and the experience of literature and poetry. This livelier multilingual language is a useful literary device but also a political and socio-cultural tool. As Ed Morales explains in his seminal book *Latinx: The New Force in American Politics and Culture*, the term Latinx "intends to describe the in-between space in which Latinx live, which allows us to cross racial boundaries more easily and construct identities, or self-images, that include a wide variety of racial, national, and even gender-based identifications". It is precisely this *in-betweenness* that has always fascinated me and drawn me to it. Morales goes even further, arguing that Latinx people are one of the primary destabilisers of Western identity: "Often erased from America's founding narratives, Latinx – in all our previous guises – have always been present as a crucial counter-narrative, a people that live in a world of many worlds, possessing an identity of multiple identities."

Being a Latinx poet born in Argentina but writing primarily within English has meant that I belong to a wider family of poets that are immersed in a multilingual, multicultural and intersectional experience: from Juan Felipe Herrera and Sandra

Cisneros, to Jorge Eduardo Eielson, Julia Alvarez, Carmen Giménez Smith and Juana Adcock, to name but a few.

As I move from one culture to another, from one memory to the next, from past to present and future, I inhabit the bilingual experience as a way of creating a sense of home (casa) and belonging (pertenencia). Bilingual poetry, and language in general for that matter, has been a sort of refuge that has allowed me to live simultaneously in many worlds at the same time, linguistically, culturally, and emotionally.

Writing Exercise

Write a poem using words from another language/s (other than English) that speak to you directly, either through personal experience (travel, partner, favourite authors, food, for example) or out of curiosity.

Try not to translate the words but give them meaning through context or just leave them as they are, exploring their musicality and sound.

Get rid of the fear of unknown languages and enrich your own poetry by exploring and discovering new foreign words, meanings, and cultural references and traditions.

KIM MOORE

Variations:
On Writing as a Feminist and Against Sexism

to notice things

I write poetry to notice things or, more accurately, I notice things because I write poetry. I notice something and wonder what it would feel like as language. I notice something and wonder what will happen to it with the white space of a poem around it. I write poems that recount the noticing of sexism. The naming of sexism often happens afterwards, when we look back, rather than in the moment. Sara Ahmed writes that "if a world can be what we learn not to notice, noticing becomes a form of political labour."Poetry as an act of noticing, as an act of political labour.

to look

I write poetry that refuses to look away. In *Ways of Seeing,* John Berger wrote: "We only see what we look at. To look is an act of choice." I look back at my experiences of sexism. I look back at my desire, and how desire and sexism are often intertwined, how female desire can call sexism into the room. I refuse to look away. I'm thinking about looking and choice and paying attention, how this looking at sexism begins to defamiliarise the world because it is not the world I thought it was. I choose to write about men, to be the wielder of the gaze, to make men the gazed upon.

because the oppressor is planted deep

Audre Lorde wrote that the focus of revolutionary change must be not only an oppressive situation, but "that piece of the oppressor which is planted deep within each of us, and which knows only the oppressors' tactics, the oppressors' relationships". I write poetry to find my own oppressor, to uncover her or, at the least, to make her smaller, or if nothing else, so I can turn away when she speaks. I write poetry to write her/root her out of me.

to raise consciousness

Whose consciousness am I trying to raise anyway? My own, my own of course; I am dredging her up. I imagine a woman with long hair emerging from black water, then sinking down again. bell hooks talked about "critical consciousness", which would allow us to see "structures of domination and how they function". Yes, even your own. I'm a structure of domination and I must learn how this works.

But also yours – your consciousness as a reader, a listener, a watcher. Back to noticing again. Back to looking again. Back to choosing. Back to oppression again, and the way we oppress ourselves and each other.

to pose a problem

It's easier to write a poem about an experience of sexism and put the framework of a lyric poem around it and use white space to elevate it or read a poem about sexism on stage to an audience of strangers than it is to sit at a table with a group of friends and talk about sexism and its impact on my daily lived experience. Sara Ahmed wrote that "when you expose a problem, you pose a problem". In my real life, I have to gather myself to pose a problem. In poetry, no gathering of the self is needed. I only have to hold on as the problem poses itself, asks me to hold it up to the light.

to use the female gaze

At the 2016 Toronto International Film Festival, Jill Soloway proposed a definition of what the female gaze might be, and how women can use it. She defined it as a "socio-political justice-demanding way of seeing" and a way of "privileging the body and emotion", and lastly, a way of "returning the gaze, not just in the act of looking back, but to say *I see you seeing me.*"

I'm writing poetry to find out how I can use the female gaze in language. How can I look at men without simply reversing our positions, how can I look at them without turning them into looking glasses, into objects?

to think about nothingness
The moments we carry with us all of our lives often have a nothingness at their heart. Why do I remember being a teenager and a man leaning forward to brush a drop of water from my thigh, when nothing else happened? Or being at infant school and being told by a teacher to close my legs? Or at a party where I was almost/not quite assaulted. (Nothing happened.) Often stories of sexism have an absence at their centre. The word 'nothing' becomes an effective protection, a wall to stop the mind imagining not only what could have happened, but also what the world might look like if these things did not keep happening.

Nothingness is a tool of the perpetrator to minimise their conduct, but it is also a tool of the victim and used to deny the importance or impact of what is happening to them, often as a coping mechanism. Virginia Woolf called these times that we carry with us, when we are suddenly jolted so we can see how the world really is "moments of being". Adrienne Rich wrote about how these moments have the power to "throw a sudden floodlight on the ways we have been living, the forces that control our lives, the hypocrisies that have allowed us to collaborate with those forces".

to find my people
If I label an event as feminist, or being about sexism, then usually only women turn up. If I give a poetry reading, there are usually men and women in the audience. I'm not interested in my poems being read only by people who already agree that sexism exists. I don't even want just to talk to people about sexism. I want to talk with them, I want to find the people I

can talk with about these things, men and women, balanced on the edge of discomfort, aware that we are all drenched in our own complicity, men and women who believe in doubt and transformation.

to write the between-us
In her book *To Be Two*, Luce Irigaray attempts to define the parameters of a relationship between two people that differs from a subject-object relationship and is instead about recognising and respecting the interiority and alterity of the other. This path between the self and another and what it might look like, and what might happen in this space, is what Irigaray calls the "between-us", and I want to write it.

to ask questions
A poem always starts with a question for me – why am I remembering this, why have I carried this for so long, what do I think about this, what do I know about this, what don't I know, what can I put into language, what can I put into silence, what can I hide with words, what can I uncover with line breaks?

Can poetry which examines sexism be new and radical, or does it invite people to re-enact the same patterns over and over again? It's exhausting to insist that sexism is real in a world which often will not admit its existence. Maybe I am asking the wrong questions. Do I trust poetry to be transformative or not? Every question I ask risks missing another part of the puzzle. Can poems raise consciousness about sexism? Can poems about sexism raise the consciousness we already have about sexism to the surface so we can talk about it? What does our consciousness around sexism look like? I could ask what transformation looks like, what does a new and liberated voice sound like, who am I talking to anyway, who am I looking at? Sexism is dynamic *and* embedded, fluid *and* static. It is all of these things. Asking questions, the wrong ones and the right ones, is an ethical, aesthetical practice.

to magnify the past

Sara Ahmed writes that "the past is magnified when it is no longer shrunk. We make things bigger just by refusing to make them smaller." Poetry can help with this of course. Experiences can be glossed over in prose – in a lyric poem, the reader is asked to pause and consider. Jonathan Culler talks about the lyric convention of significance: "the fact that something has been set down as a poem implies that it is important now, at the moment of articulation, however trivial it might seem".

The white space around a poem, as well as making the content harder to minimise or discount, also signifies silence, the place where language has failed in some way, the place where time makes its presence felt. The structure of the lyric poem, its inherent framework, supports magnification of events with nothing at their heart. We are back to nothingness again.

to combine the personal, political and social

In her introduction to the anthology *Against Forgetting: Twentieth-Century Poetry of Witness*, Carolyn Forché argued for a new kind of poetry that combined the personal, the political and the social, coining the term "poetry of witness". Whilst most of the poems in the anthology dealt with extreme trauma and experiences of war, I would like to expand the definition of "poetry of witness" to include poems that examine experiences of sexism and gender-based violence and misogyny. These experiences show how the personal is invaded by both the political and the social.

There is space for the lyric poem to be a potent, radical and change-making space in which to discuss experiences of sexism. One possibility, outlined by Jonathan Culler, is to revision the lyric as it was once thought of in ancient Greece – as "discourse that aims to praise or persuade – as epideictic discourse".

to be an intimate witness

I first read the phrase "intimate witness" in an essay by the poet Mary Jean Chan, who was discussing the work of Claudia Rankine. Chan points out that, in her book *Citizen*, Rankine becomes an "intimate witness" of racial injustice through her use of micro-observation and refusal to look away from insidious trauma. These techniques invite the reader to think about the wider implications of the small-scale social scenes that she documents.

I want to take the material of individual interactions and use poetry to transform these into social knowledge. I must be an intimate witness of myself. I must be an intimate witness of you.

to write of desire

I am writing poems of desire. I want you to wonder how much desire one life can hold.

to find out what lyric poetry is for

Lyric poetry as documentation, as biography of violence, as feminist work. Lyric poetry as testimony, as intimate witnessing. Lyric poetry as social engagement, as epideictic discourse, as persuasion, as praise, as a path from past to present, from present to past. Lyric poetry as relational, as between us, as a way of looking. Lyric poetry as micro-observation, as experiential, as personal, as political, as social, as rooted in history, as a repeating moment in time, as a way of generating empathy. Lyric poetry as beautiful failure, as container of silence, as holder of symbol, of image. Lyric poetry as transformation for the reader, for the writer. Lyric as the place where nothing transforms at all.

to be wilful and willing

Do you know the Grimms' fairy tale of the wilful girl? She does not do as she is told, so eventually God allows her to become ill and she dies. Even in death, her arm rises from the grave, until her mother takes a rod and beats it. Sara Ahmed writes that the tale of the wilful girl is addressed to the willing girl.

Maybe there is no such thing as a 'wilful' woman/girl or a 'willing' woman/girl. In real life, women are composites of both of these figures and we move between the two of them consciously and unconsciously. I want my poems to address the wilful/willing woman and call her to attention. I want the call to wilfulness/willingness to be a call both to the body and to language.

 Writing Exercise

Illuminated Moments
Think of a moment in your past, maybe from childhood, that you have carried with you. It should be an unexplained memory, one where you are not quite clear why it is significant. Write a poem about it which lights up that moment. Send yourself back there, using all of your senses to explore it, but don't consciously try and work out the significance. Let that emerge through the writing.

Think about what you know, and what you don't know, about why you've remembered this for so long. How has having this memory inside you all these years changed you, shaped you? Put that into the poem.

Sometimes mining the past can be painful, particularly if it is a traumatic memory. If this is the case for you, make sure you've got support for when you finish writing.

KEITH JARRETT

Hymning from the Sing Sheet: On the Power and Performance of Writing Poetry

1.

I owe my throat to the slam scene; not my whole voice, but part of it.

Experiencing your own words as they land in the ears of an audience can be exhilarating, terrifying or both. The added pressure of time restrictions and competition intensifies this already exposing feat, as the words you've composed face the judgement of the audience. In offering up my vulnerability to a crowd for three minutes – and returning to the stage time and again – I've also learned the power of speaking out loud beyond the world of poetry.

In the past, I've described slams – and live literature, in general – as a religious rite, although that probably speaks more to my upbringing; we harvest the metaphors we have closest to hand. What I really meant is that being in the same room – or virtual space – as your audience, being *heard*, and allowing for real-time communication, is precious. And that which is most precious is often the least appreciated.

How many times has spoken word been denied, disavowed by poets who want to be taken "seriously"? Perhaps that specific question is for another day; however, restrictions on live performance due to the coronavirus pandemic have given me time to reflect more on why I perform, and what is missed when your voice can only be released onto the page. The intention of this piece, then, is to provoke reflections on the *what* and the *whys* before moving on to thinking about *how* to make a performance sing.

2.

Before continuing, several acknowledgments, in an instinctual order:

- My working definition: *performance* is a visual, three-dimensional manifestation of poetry.
- Contradictions may occur throughout this piece.
- Performance poetry is not a parallel dimension of poetry; just like sexuality, *performativity* and *visual/concrete* do not exist on a binary, but rather on a continuum.
- Translated: 'Page' and 'Stage' is an artificial distinction.
- Language that is spoken is amorphous. If this were a conversation, I might gauge reactions, pause, allow interjections, protestation …
- If this were a performance, I could navigate irony, double entendre and earnestness simply through intonation of my voice or the curl of a lip.
- You can read the same poem twice, but you will rarely hear a poem performed live the same way twice.
- If I read this piece aloud, I might change the emphasis the second time around: you *can* read the same … you can *read* the same …
- *Heard* is intended inclusively. British Sign Language exists. International slams are often captioned. The emphasis is on the *live* communication between author and audience.
- This essay is a conversation, or perhaps a performance.
- A performance *is* a conversation, even when the audience is silent. A gasp, a sigh, a split second of eye contact, or just the simple acknowledgment of a shared length of time … The emphasis is on *shared*.
- Poetry involves sharing, intimacy. Yes, some poets eschew the lyrical *I*, but it is no coincidence that most live poetry is personal, self-reflective.
- This involves two-way consent. I am concerned, lately, with managing this unwritten contract between poet and listener, the contract that demands of the audience: "I want

you to hear me, to lend me your time." It also demands reciprocity from the poet, and responsibility for holding the audience's attention.

- Working definition: *live literature* is the manipulation of words, sound and time.
- It is also embodied. If you know me, chances are, you're reading this in my voice. Chances are the intent of my words would land differently if I appeared before you now: a racialised, sexualised, classed, gendered, generationally packaged being. We take our cues from the visual: the subtle differences in our clothes, the shape of our Ts, the roundness of our vowels. *Text vs. context vs. subtexts etc …*
- It's not my place to reinvent the wheel; I'm just here to spoke a little.
- Puns work better live than on the page, but they work best as first draft cast-offs.
- Whenever I memorise a poem, it absorbs into my sinews, fuses into my marrow.
- Whenever I speak a poem, I relive it, rewrite it.
- I am not an authority on any of this. (Who is?)
- Recent years have seen – overdue – academic analysis of live performance.
- Live performance has changed considerably, will continue to change. Whatever I say now will be up for debate in under a generation.
- The suggested duration for reading this list is three minutes. Points will be deducted if you exceed the time.

3.

The above declarations may sound unstructured, or like a freestyle; reflecting on our practice involves reaching across time, across spaces. Performance is a disorderly beast, a tangle of leads trailing up to a mic.

My impulse in the first instance is to navigate the territory of the poet-performer in ways that tease out the originality of this tradition, using my own instinct, my own body as guide.

To perform means to place the whole self in the picture, in a way that writing alone cannot.

The 'performance poet' or 'spoken word poet' – choose the epithet that best fits – operates in a physical space, be it stage, upstairs pub-lounge or bedroom-turned-broadcast studio. This physicality erases some of the distance between *writer*-self and embodied self. I can't just be vulnerable on my own at home; I need to engage with an audience on their terms, even if via the internet. It would be too trite to suggest a unique *truth* here, but there is a certain earnestness in appearing before listeners with a handful of words and nothing else: no music, no theatre, little other adornment.

The nakedness of the form makes poetry more versatile, more of an equaliser than other arts, other sports; ideas are the only requirement. In theory, this should make it more accessible across class and gender lines. In practice, those of us who feel more entitled to speak will find ourselves at the top of the list.

4.
Now follows a few words for the *whys*:

Before taking a platform, we must map the landscape. *Why do I feel the need to be heard? Who am I not hearing/hearing enough … and why?* Such unsettling questions for the gut!

Before signing up to speak aloud, I always ask: what can I offer that isn't already being said? Sometimes when I do this the question rankles; there are *living* poets, from my own city, who can articulate the human experience better than I can ever hope to, let alone those further afield, or dead, who can be pulled up on a screen with a swiping thumb. Even so, this is an empowering rather than a humiliating exercise, for four reasons:

- Acknowledging this from the outset relieves the pressure. It's not your responsibility to say the most profound thing ever. At best, you will connect with an audience member, just for a moment. Maybe the performance will be filmed, you'll go viral and will appear as an ... *and finally* story. Maybe that *one* line was particularly memorable for someone. You can relax, breathe easy.
- Secondly, it relieves the pressure. Even if you fluff your lines, mumble, get heckled, or soil your pants as you speak, you'll likely live to perform another day.
- Thirdly, it sets a challenge. If it doesn't make any difference to you, you shouldn't be writing – let alone performing – poetry. Competing in slams, or similar competitive formats, is one way to push yourself. You may not want to emulate the world's most celebrated poets, but you should hope your words resonate like theirs do. If it's been said before, you may want to dig deeper into your own experience, your unique way of harvesting the imagination.
- Fourthly: I'm hesitant to employ the word *authenticity* as it's too often wielded clumsily. But while the idea of poems transcending time and space does have some merit, the performed word is powerful precisely because it's rooted in time and space, something that can be leaned into. If even *living* poets in my city are speaking about love, justice, or what it means to be black and queer in the twenty-first century, or aliens, tower blocks, or whatever else I feel compelled to explore, I can a) approach it from an even more precise angle and/or b) speak with even more intention, drawing from specific memories, or perhaps just altering my performance to include elements that are only relevant to that audience on that day.

5.

Authenticity demands risk-taking.

The first poems I ever performed were about travelling on the Tube, or themes I deemed universal. I rarely disclosed anything about myself. I felt *safe,* or at least safer, this way. I didn't see many examples around me of people speaking the poems I wanted to speak, although I had started experimenting with writing that felt risky. Transitioning from writing dangerously to performing dangerously isn't always an easy one. Dipping your toes in the water helps, and three methods spring to mind:

i. The penultimate poem test... When invited to feature at an event, perform whatever you know will be a hit. Start with a banger, end with a favourite but, in between – having warmed up the listeners, but before ending on a tried and tested poem – use this space to experiment.

ii. The substitution test... You will never *same* the performed poem twice, so why not make some deliberate choices *just once*? You can always change it back next time!

iii. The pre-record... Practice in front of a mirror, including your pre-amble (if you must qualify your poem before you speak it). Record yourself. A risky poem spoken confidently is much stronger than a solid poem that doesn't fit the mouth right.

6.

The mouth, the throat, the tongue...? It's perfectly possible to think that performance resides in the head, even though I've discussed *embodiment* a few times, even though I've addressed all the steps leading up to the performance. I've completely omitted to talk about the feet and the chest, where this exploration will land, where we'll find our raisons d'être.

A spoken word poet needs to breathe right for the poem to really *sing*. Musicians, especially vocalists, know this. Actors know this. *Comedians* know this. So much of how a poem lands depends on timing. On breath. On how and when we choose to push the words through our lips. If we're not in a good relationship with our diaphragms, we may run into problems. We'll find ourselves cutting up the lines all wrong. The poem won't flow well.

I can say nothing here that an online tutorial can't expand on better. A good vocal warm-up – of which there are plenty – will help you work those lungs as best as you can.

7.

I owe my life to poetry… sort of. These 'owing' phrases need a qualifier. Poetry is a vital part of my existence but isn't the totality of it. Language helps interpret our experience of the world, to push against it through rhymes, metaphor, etc. Performance is one method to convey this and, paradoxically, one way to listen.

Too often, audiences and performers alike interpret the live form's nakedness as unskilfulness, rather than as an alchemy of literature and orality. It risks being seen as just a stepping stone to other glitzy forms: music, theatre or multimedia performance. But as its own discrete community – and a politically engaged one, at that – it can be revolutionary.

Performance, like teaching, is a reminder that I'm part of something bigger; writing alone feels like a withdrawal into myself. Both are necessary, like inhaling and exhaling.

After teaching spoken word poetry to teenagers over the years, I'm less afraid of being judged by adults. (Year 8 girls should be detectives; their powers of observation are unsurpassable.) I used to stand on my tiptoes as I was performing, which I guess was my way of dealing with nerves and pushing my voice out, but I have learned to put both feet on the ground, to still myself and own what I say without apology, head to toe. The greatest thing performance has taught me is how to allow poetry to move through the whole body.

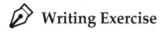 **Writing Exercise**

Inhabiting the Body
This two-step exercise may help you to think about working a poem through your body and is designed to encourage self-reflection. Each poem is different – so the tasks may work better for some poems than others. Try completing one or both tasks with any poem and experiment!

Step 1: Balance Sheet
Print out a copy of your poem. Underline up to three important lines that are most crucial to unlocking the poem's meaning. How can you underline their importance with your *performance*? Are there any ways that sounds or non-verbal communication might step in?

Some options: repeat the line for emphasis; slow down your delivery during these lines; insert a pause before and/or after the line; increase your volume; punctuate the lines with an action, a gasp, a laugh …

Once you've decided on your technique, you are going to have to provide a counterbalance. Is there a less important line that you can shorten or erase completely, or find ways to make pacier? The trick is to 'balance out' the poem!

Step 2: Body Audit
Practise your poem and film yourself, or get someone else to film you, making sure the recording captures your whole body. Play it back and make notes. Where are your feet? Where are your hands? How do you move your head, your face, your position over the course of the poem?

Tip: if it's more useful this way – and if you can handle watching yourself several times – watch only your feet the first time; the second time, focus on any hand/body movements; finally, zoom in on your face.

When you next practise the poem, focus on your stance; feel the poem moving through your feet. Be deliberate with any movements you make, paying particular attention to what you've noticed from the recordings.

ROSIE GARLAND

Don't Fence Me In: On Writing Across Genres

"Diversify" (Iggy Pop)
In my beginning was the word. As an adopted child (an unwanted girl) I grew up with a keen sense of difference.

There was a lot of 'othering', not limited to sexuality, but in every way going. I felt like an alien. As an isolated, geeky kid, I went through an (understandable) stage of fearing there was something wrong with me.

I turned to books. Between their pages I discovered the imaginative potential for a world where oddities as myself could live and thrive. Books introduced the radical notion difference is okay. It didn't have to be terrifying. It was who I was.

Nurtured by public libraries, I read voraciously, hungry for elsewheres and elsewhens where I might build a place of belonging. From fairy tales to *Alice in Wonderland*, E. A. Poe to e e cummings, *Asterix* to *Beowulf*, folk ballads to Frank Zappa, science fiction to science fact, *Conan the Barbarian* to the Brontës, I drank in the power of language, and there was always room for more.

I didn't just devour, I created. Stories for my toys (they were good listeners), histories and geographies of invented places, angst-ridden poetry, nonsense songs, and all of it created with the freewheeling energy of a child, unshackled by any inner critic (she came later).

"[N]ever lose interest, never grow indifferent – lose your invaluable curiosity and you let yourself die. It's as simple as that." (Tove Jansson)

It won't come as any surprise to hear I'm drawn to the liminal: that which exists on the edges – both time and space and those who live there, either by design or through circumstance. Outsiders, people who don't/can't fit and are fed up trying to force themselves into the restrictive and frankly unimaginative templates society offers. Folk who slide under the radar, and never make it into the history books (which is all of us, right?). Whose stories have been marginalised and overlooked.

I travel diverse paths: mischievous, inventive and questioning. There's more than one side to a story and innumerable ways to tell it. No single book has every answer, or indeed the only answer (though I kept this to myself when a convent girl). 'Outskirts' depends on where you're standing. 'Outsider' is an opinion, imposed by those who regard themselves as 'inside', and impose their arbitrary norms. As every queer knows, "Heterosexuality is not normal, it's just common" (Dorothy Parker).

"I contain multitudes" (Walt Whitman)

I find the interest in everything. I've heard this expansive, passionate curiosity described as 'Renaissance wo/man'. I prefer the term multiplicity. I write to explore a multiplicity of interests, for a multiplicity of reasons, in a multiplicity of forms. Woolf describes the concept of possessing multiple potentialities in *Orlando*: "How many different people are there … having lodgement at one time or another in the human spirit? Some say two thousand and fifty-two."

On the face of it, multiplicity could come over as confusing: a babel clamour for attention; a pinball machine of clanging bells and flashing lights; ideas spinning in unmanageable directions, fizzling out in cinders and ash.

And breathe.

Rather than chaos, I experience connection. I have conversations with myself (or rather, selves), resulting in disparate creative expressions. Some forms seem better suited than others when expressing certain ideas.

I'll illustrate with two of a possible myriad of examples:

When writing a novel (e.g. *The Night Brother* – Borough Press, 2017), I plunge into the secret lives of a group of individuals. At times it feels like a lengthy and ardent affair, where I'm impatient to sneak away and spend time with the characters.

At the other end of the scale, my performance persona, Rosie Lugosi the Lesbian Vampire Queen, embodies the flamboyant intersection of the Gothic, feminism, comedy, deviance and the queer, none of which are supposed to exist in the same room, let alone the same person.

Woolf again: "These selves of which we are built up ... have attachments elsewhere, sympathies, little constitutions and rights of their own ... one will only come if it is raining, another in a room with green curtains, another when Mrs Jones is not there, another if you can promise it a glass of wine ..."

I find beauty and excitement in writing from different perspectives. Rather than exerting rigid control, forcing creativity to behave properly and toe other people's lines, I let go and write. With the help of a notebook beside the bed, or recording voice notes while walking, I permit "the buzz of meteors that tumble down the sky" ('Exit Ophelia'). I venture into possibilities, and relish the fluidity.

Being 'in the flow', if you will. The categorisation comes after. Everything sorts itself neatly into boxes labelled poem, novel, lyric, short story.

Oh, wait. Sometimes it doesn't.

Take 'The Correct Hanging of Game Birds'. First published in *X–R-A-Y Magazine* (mission statement *'to publish uncomfortable, entertaining, unforgettable prose'*), it features in the poetry collection *What Girls Do in the Dark* (Nine Arches Press, 2020), and was selected for Best Microfiction 2021. Similarly, 'Perihelion is the closest a comet gets to the fire before managing to escape' (in the same collection) was first published in *Extra Teeth* as an essay. The editors said, "We don't know what it is, but we like it."

Does that make these pieces charlatans and cheats? Are they cuckoos in the poetic nest, elbowing out true poems? Or do they broaden the range of what poetry can be, can encompass? Even more tantalising, do they represent the intersection of poetry and quantum mechanics? Quantum theory suggests this is not as far-fetched as it may seem.

Here's the science:

"Six impossible things before breakfast" (The White Queen, Through the Looking-Glass, and What Alice Found There by Lewis Carroll.)
Prepare for a swift warp ride around the weird and wonderful world of quantum superposition. Briefly, the notion of matter existing in different quantum states at the same time. A popular example is Schrödinger's cat, a slippery and elusive feline, simultaneously dead and alive. It only becomes 'fixed' in one state at the moment of observation and measuring.

I see no reason why this theory can't be applied to writing. While creating, I permit words to exist as potentialities in multiple states. The piece settles into poem, flash, lyric essay, and so on, when fixed by a reader, for example. Sometimes. My writing has a tendency to inhabit in-between states – often termed hybrid – where I allow it to possess the fluid capacity to be different things at the same time, without the need to come down on one side.

I can't help thinking of Fitzgerald's words: "The test of a first-rate intelligence is the ability to hold two opposing ideas in mind at the same time and still retain the ability to function" (F. Scott Fitzgerald, *The Crack-Up*).

Why limit oneself to two?

Perhaps writing is the long-sought Grand Unifying Theory of Everything.

"Don't Fence Me In" (Cole Porter)
As someone who eludes rigid definitions in their personal life, it seems appropriate for my writing to follow suit. I'm fired up by poetry that reconsiders its potential and explores what it can be, rather than what we are told it ought to be.

A lived experience of not-fitting has cultivated an awareness of the limitations and inadequacy of labels. Sure, they're useful in their place (*Kids! Put milk on your cornflakes, not depleted uranium!*). I'm wary of the tendency of categorisation to harden into boundaries, which can both imprison and exclude. Oscar Wilde said "to define is to limit" (*The Picture of Dorian Gray*), and he knew a thing or two about prisons.

This is not the same as uncertainty or ambivalence (or, heaven forbid, laziness). I'm passionately certain of who I am. Steeped in the power and discipline of form, I'm equally certain of the words chosen for a piece: their beat, depth of meaning, rhythm, sound, texture. Whatever the form – and it may be hybrid and unfitting – my desire is to disrupt/breach barriers, and speak across borders.

"I write entirely to find out what I'm thinking, what I'm looking at, what I see and what it means." (Joan Didion)
I write to communicate, in a spirit of adventuring out as well as in. I don't always know the end of a poem or novel at the start, but I am learning to trust I'll find something, whatever it may be.

Everything is connected and I write to connect. If you can cope with a smidgeon more science, this is a fair summary of the First Law of Thermodynamics (and the theme of my poem, 'Now that you are not-you'). Poetry is a place I go to for communion, to create a bridge between writer and reader. I wish to welcome the reader in, and give them space to have their own thoughts.

Dammit, I want space for my own thoughts.

I write to ask myself questions. Not to hammer answers flat, but to explore the questions via the reflection poetry enables and allows. To discover what I think and how that changes, develops and grows. With each poem, flash or novel, I challenge myself to go somewhere I haven't been before. A different corner of the geography.

"Action is the antidote to despair" (Joan Baez)
Writing is often pitched as the opposite of action. Clearly, I disagree. If words are so inert and unthreatening, how come history is littered with acts of violence wreaked on those who dare to read (Malala Yousafzai, 2012), speak out (Malcolm X, 1965), or spread the word (Tyndale, 1536)?

Through writing, I practise and enact my right to speak. Writing is belief in action: my words are worthy of expression. They and I have a right to take up space: queer, female, working class, and the whole damn thing.

Writing is a way through. Putting one word in front of the other is an act of perseverance. It helps me (re)connect with myself and the world. It is the balancing pole grasped by the tightrope walker to steady herself on the high wire.

'Enjoy Yourself (It's Later than You Think)' (Herb Magidson)

Finally, one of my favourite multiplicities is to permit joy. Poetry – reading and writing – nourishes and supports through tough times. There is so much to make us miserable that any avenues to joy are worth highlighting. It's easy to spin away from the still, small voice of hope and become swallowed up in doomscrolling, which feeds despair and saps what little energy we have for the struggle.

Audre Lorde said, "Poetry is not a luxury". Neither is joy a luxury we're only allowed to feel when "everything is perfect". It is a radical act. "Joy doesn't betray but sustains activism. And when you face a politics that aspires to make you fearful, alienated and isolated, joy is a fine act of insurrection" (Rebecca Solnit, *Hope in the Dark*).

And if comparison is "the thief of joy" (Theodore Roosevelt) or "the death of joy" (Mark Twain), then connection constitutes its life and nourishment. Hope and joy are vital for existence.

There's a cliché: poets write because they want to live forever. I write because I want to – need to – consider the fact I won't. Through writing, I explore the nature of my flicker. I plan to pack the time between now and then with as much creative expression as possible.

> I turn to words.
> Their little lamps will outlive my flicker,
> that of lords, and of this current fear. I grind
> gall, vinegar, hone my quill. Feed the dark age with light.
> ('Bede writes a history of the English people')

Writers have an urgent, exciting task. Our stories have value and are important, even when weird and ill-fitting. Especially when weird and ill-fitting. Times are tough. The time we have is short. Time is all we have. Do it now.

 Writing Exercise

Collision can be productive rather than destructive. Take two problematic/unfinished pieces and collide them with each other. Explore the questions they ask of each other.

This was how the Beatles wrote 'A Day in the Life'. And they transformed the history of popular music.

ZAFFAR KUNIAL

Beginnings and Prayer:
On Connecting People, Time and Place

My poem 'Prayer' begins with the word *first* and, like many
of my poems, it is a search for a beginning. In the process of
writing it, unexpectedly, it became about endings, and about
the last words I had said to my mother before she died – a
subject that I hadn't begun to write about directly until it arose
in this poem. The only other reference to my mother's death
was in a poem called 'Poppy', where, like the flower, it crops
up unexpectedly.

I had expected the 'Prayer' poem to be about language primarily
and was vaguely aiming to forge a connection between George
Herbert's poem 'Prayer (I)' and my father's first words to me
as a baby, whispered into my ear, the Arabic words Allah hu
Akbar. Evoking a distant land, Herbert's final line is: "The land
of spices; something understood."

These are the last items in his list-like sonnet made of metaphors
or definitions of what prayer is, and I had an initiating idea
to write about the foreignness of first words, and how those I
received were in a language that wasn't native to myself or my
father, and then perhaps also, as a secondary subject, the idea
of listening as a kind of faraway *first place*.

Digression: *First*
According to a word cloud computed from the manuscript
for my first full poetry collection, *Us*, the word I used the
most – words such as *the, and*, etc. aren't included – was *first*.
This wasn't planned or a consciously repeated usage of the
word, *first*. I think it reflects an inner obsession that comes to
the surface during composition to source an origin, or even

to ask whether a beginning in space or time is possible to locate. *Where do I begin?* seems to be the question I'm asking, even when I think I'm addressing a particular subject in the foreground that stands more groundedly apart from that question. Had I known how prominent this obsession was I might have resisted it consciously, but I can see that the unknown obsession asserts itself almost from one of my first or earliest confusions – from a dimly remembered time before I could articulate the feeling behind the cloudy interjection – *where do I begin?*

The place of this question is itself difficult to locate but does seem in its hazy way to be a driving force, to have a kind of power. Perhaps this relates to what Wordsworth meant when he wrote of "the hiding places of my power" – but for me, this power is not obviously assertive or even mine, but that of a wavering confusion that feels like the opposite of any power or control: something misunderstood, that might even sabotage my attempts to write, even while it also drives them. A back-seat driver bent on digressing, and on repeating certain journeys, but unsure of the road ahead or behind. A *first* feeling, positioned in a shy, uncertain hiding place.

Returning to 'Prayer'

The position of the ear as a liminal zone also became a focus of the poem as I wrote it. In Islamic tradition, the father whispers into the right ear of a newborn baby, and my father proudly told me on many occasions that this had happened, a story that was often followed by an account of how long the birth process was. My mother's waters broke on Friday and I was born the following Monday, doing a full rotation in the womb in the process, and being born blue and having fits that led the doctors to do a lumbar puncture to withdraw spinal fluid to test for meningitis and then to keep me in an incubator. My father spoke of praying in the waiting room before and following my birth. Decades later, when my mother was diagnosed with cancer, hours before she died earlier that same day, I said to her that the last time I was on a hospital bed with her would have been during my birth.

In my poem I quote the full line of Herbert, wanting to almost make his line part of the same breath as lines in my poem: "God's breath in man returning to his birth". Having the line in my poem made me think of that last day of my mother's life, of her last breaths, and us having spoken earlier that day about my difficult birth. The ear I began writing about – my own first hearings – moved towards my mother's ear – and perhaps the last words she heard. I wrote this draft on a train between Leeds and Hebden Bridge and the time disappeared as I wrote it, partly through my engagement with it and the shock of writing about a buried moment I hadn't planned to write about. I remember walking through Hebden Bridge, looking for a café to sit in and read it again, partly to steady myself and partly to edit the poem.

The first draft was, unusually for me, in an almost finished state. What changed more than the content of the poem was the shape and the sound patterning. There were many feminine endings in the poem – particularly, it seemed to me, sounds which linked with the word *her*:

Akbar, father, ear, her, earth, birth, hear(d).

Not only had the poem moved from my ear to my mother's ear across time, it also went from a masculine distant God, and a personal father, to a mother and a feminine receiver of prayers, as well as from a distant foreign language to intimate English. The close resemblance of the sounds around the word *her* gather these distances together in a communion around a kind of hearing or *hereing*. The *her* in *Herbert* and then in *Hereford* add to this coincidental confluence that draws distance into the unified present of an ear. In editing the poem, I added the words *hurt* and *hurl* to draw the reader back and forward to these sounds that chime in the end of the word *prayer* and hint perhaps at the endlessness of the audience of prayer. I was thinking about the idea of ends, or the final *earth* of prayer. Herbert's rhyme of *birth* and *earth* sonically and economically suggest the beginnings and endings of life being drawn into one, within the ear at least.

In Herbert's poem, prayer is also "angels' age" and "Reversed thunder" – two concepts which play with the scale and direction of human time and transcendent time. A hearing beyond Earth or the earthly is hinted at in the closing couplet of Herbert's poem: "Church-bells beyond the stars heard, the soul's blood, / The land of spices; something understood."

The final phrase, after the suggested foreignness of "[t]he land of spices", is matter-of-fact and earthy, an inhabiting of distance: "something understood".

This phrase feels appropriate also for the thud of knowledge that comes with watching a person's death, the internalisation that this is the end of life. A thud in the blood, as another heart stops. The rhyme of *blood* and *understood* compresses distance, and within myself I am aware that my parental ancestry or *blood* compresses difference, as my mother's and father's means of being *understood*, their primary language, was also very different.

Through negotiation with Herbert's poem and with the themes of my own, many types of distance became encompassed in the poem I was writing. With Herbert, as with his fellow metaphysical poet John Donne, the encompassing of distance is not only a figurative theme but also a kind of poetics, where thought and emotion are ideally drawn together through words which collectively work on different levels in a well-wrought line. In my poem, the idea of a line is also the lineage of poetry, how one line of thought can be brought into the present and even continued beyond the death of the poet's time: "If I continued // his lines from there."

The enjambed stanza visually represents the double break involved. The word *his* not only contrasts with the word *her* but also complicates the idea of who is speaking, meaning first Herbert's line, but more distantly hints at referring back to a masculine God in the quoted line, "God's breath in man returning to his birth". Reading Herbert's 'Prayer (I)', it seems significant to me that Herbert made his sonnet of one continuous line, and I imagine this must have been because Herbert felt that breaking the sentence was ill-suited to his theme. This large stretching sentence is achieved partly through the use of semi-colons that act as bridges, pausing but not breaking the thought. And this stretch is also the theme of my poem 'Prayer', between two ears, a continuous *here* and hearing.

The final word of my poem, *heard*, echoes the place name of Hereford, and also the finality and some of the meaning of *understood* in Herbert's poem, though with far greater uncertainty and a feminine addressee: "I won't know if she heard."

The point at which a dying person loses hearing is uncertain. Similarly, the beginning of hearing as humans is difficult to locate – should it be sounds in the womb whenever hearing develops, or should it be located after the shock and division of birth, when the hearing separates from the body of the mother? My poem starts with: "First heard words ..." So the poem begins with a confident statement of words being heard, and heard first. Yet this is obviously contentious. The intention of my father was certainly to speak the first words into his newborn baby's ear. Perhaps the separation involved in birth from the mother's body is aligned here with the idea of vocal sounds becoming separate *words* – separate words intentionally directed to the separate listener. Perhaps here there is a link being made between the space before birth, with the space after death, a space where words cannot be separate or heard separately.

I am reminded of a poem that I have read many times as I find it intriguing in relation to the notion of continuous hearing, a poem I realise now maybe links for me with the idea of prayer and, also, of the womb – Wallace Stevens' 'Tea at the Palaz of Hoon', and these last lines in particular:

> What were the hymns that buzzed beside my ears?
> What was the sea whose tide swept through me there?
>
> Out of my mind the golden ointment rained,
> And my ears made the blowing hymns they heard.
> I was myself the compass of that sea:
>
> I was the world in which I walked, and what I saw
> Or heard or felt came not but from myself;
> And there I found myself more truly and more strange.

This poem is from a collection called *Harmonium* and the book's title also chimes for me with the idea of a continuum that is sonically based. Stevens' poem was not at all on my mind as I wrote my poem, but it seems to resonate deeply and was a poem I read many times a decade earlier, when I first encountered it. I realise that locating the creative impulses of a poem at the time of writing it, and in what one is consciously aware of at that time, can only at best tell part of the story. Writing now about the process of the poem, it seems that I am encountering connections that may have been hidden impulses. The line I was most intrigued by in Stevens' poem – "And my ears made the blowing hymns they heard" – hints at the looping nature of creativity, of hymns, and the ear as a site of birth or making. Whether or not this intrigue was a hidden element behind my creative 'process', the very theme of a looping continuum, as represented by the ear, is closely pertinent to my poem 'Prayer'.

Another line from Stevens, "I was myself the compass of that sea", now makes me think of the kind of prenatal hearing a baby might have in the womb. On the day my mother died I compared the sound of her oxygen machine to the sound of the sea. I did this because I remembered that my mother said once that she found the rhythm of the sea reassuring and almost mother-like. When I told my mother about the oxygen machine sounding "like the sea", I could not hear her reply. She took off her oxygen mask to repeat the words but again I couldn't hear them. I then put my ear close to her mouth and she said, faintly, two words: "No rhythm."

As I was writing the 'Prayer' poem, this memory was beneath the floorboards, so to speak. The connections of breaths, first and last, to the heart monitor ("time and rhythm flatlining") were aroused by the line from Herbert – "God's breath in man, returning to his birth". The idea of continuation with the mother's body being linked to poetic continuation through remembered lines of verse was also there. This memory can be consciously remembered lines, or perhaps a more distant memory to do with sound or a dim sense of energetic connection with what otherwise has been forgotten. This recalls what T.S. Eliot wrote about the *auditory imagination*: "the feeling for syllable and rhythm, penetrating far below the conscious levels of thought and feeling … sinking to the most primitive and forgotten, returning to the origin and bringing something back, seeking the beginning and the end".

The auditory continuum across space and time, its presence and its entropic breakage, is evoked in 'Prayer' by the way my poem separates within its lines towards the end:

> by midnight her rings were off.
>
> I stayed on. At her bed.
> Earlier, time and rhythm flatlining, I whispered
> *Thank you   I love you   thank you*
>
> mouth at her ear.
> She stared on, ahead. I won't know if she heard.

The words "her bed" refer to the death bed in Hereford hospital, but might also be read as signifying the bed referred to originally, where my mother gave birth to me. That "her bed" chimes with *Herbert* perhaps amplifies a secondary auditory link to the way a poet's words may bed into a future poetic line or bed themselves in future consciousness. The lacunae or gaps in the penultimate line add to the sense both of breakage but also of a distance being forded at a time when the ultimate break in consciousness, death, is happening. Prayer in general is perhaps the attempt to speak across distance until it collapses when speech fords the ultimate gap between the known and the unknown.

 ## Writing Exercise

Think of two of your own poems that you like but are very different, and seemingly worlds apart – and try to begin something which could sit between each of the poems somehow and connect their worlds.

This essay is based on a PhD thesis extract from: 'Fromwards: Wavering Between Beginnings' by Zaffar Kunial.

DANIEL SLUMAN

How I Built a New Voice:
On Writing and Living as a Disabled Poet

Finding your voice is talked about so much within the world of writing it's become something of a cliché. Ironically though, very little has been written about the process; the implication being that finding your voice is a one-off task that once achieved need never be thought of again. It's as if the voice is an object we lift from the mantelpiece before sitting down to write. But what if your voice is no longer fit for purpose? What if you fall into rhythms of speech and syntax that are more a representation of what you read than who you are or what you want to say? In this essay, I'd like to discuss the process of building my voice from scratch to suit one specific project: my third collection of poetry. My hope is that this self-analysis may encourage others to reflect on how they can improve the ways they explore and represent themselves on the page.

Like most writers, my voice developed through reading, writing, and learning as much as I could about craft early on in my career. By the time my second collection came out I had struck upon a way of expressing myself that was consistent, but as much as I was happy with my work up until that point, I knew I had to approach my next collection differently. I am an amputee with chronic pain, and my wife has fibromyalgia and Crohn's disease, and due to our disabilities, we spent much of the time between 2015 and 2017 confined to the sofa in our living room, and, later, between the sofa and the bedroom, when fatigue sent our sleep cycles in opposing directions. I had written a number of poems about disability before that point, but I felt compelled to explore this difficult period my wife and I faced, during a time when the Tories introduced a raft of controversial policies against disabled people which sadly continue to this day. I wanted to give justice to the pain, isolation and fear myself and my wife experienced, and I knew I had to create a new voice and a new poetics to do this.

I began my process by studying the possibilities for change shown in the output of two favourite poets. In 1957, Robert Lowell couldn't help but notice the rise in popularity of the Beat poets, and the way archaic language and traditional forms were being dismantled for spontaneity and directness instead. He could see the limitations inherent in the style of his poems like 'A Quaker Graveyard in Nantucket', which often used tight iambic forms. Lowell found himself simplifying the diction and language of many of these poems as he read them on the road, and this sonic refinement lead to a shift in ideology from the muscular poems about Catholicism found in *Lord Weary's Castle* to the loose, adjective-heavy imagery of his family history in *Life Studies*. Much to the surprise of critics and peers, Lowell had moved with the currents of contemporary poetry and created a voice in this period of time that pleased existing readers and brought him many new ones too.

Ted Hughes may have pivoted his voice even more wildly than Lowell. His accessible, naturalistic tone was relatively even throughout most of his career, but he changed everything in *Crow*. In this book, there is a carnivalesque exploration of mortality through the experiences of a trickster-style character that sometimes uses Old Testament-style rhetoric and language bordering on the cartoon-like. *Birthday Letters* marked another evolutionary change – the tone became more personal and carefully metered out, as Hughes reminisced on his time with Sylvia Plath using lines that seemed to melt one into the other.

*

After my second collection, I entered a self-enforced silence for a couple of years. This meant putting on hold the cycle of writing, revising, and submitting to journals that seems to be the default mode for poets. The process of writing and publication (which I'm tremendously privileged to be part of) had come along again so quickly after launching my first book in 2012 that I felt off balance and creatively out of breath when it happened again by 2015. In entering this 'reset' period afterwards, I allowed myself to seriously think about the voice I had developed (or fallen into) and how I might better represent my disability and personal experiences through my future poetry.

There is a woeful lack of critical research and resources on disability poetry, but one name you're guaranteed to come across is Larry Eigner. Learning about Eigner in my PhD was a revelation. Here was a disabled poet with cerebral palsy who was not side-lined as a 'disabled poet', but accepted by the mainstream. A Black Mountain Poet, Eigner published over forty books, and used the page to *think* through his ideas in a way heavily influenced by Charles Olson's now famous 'Projective Verse'. His poems utilise the page differently: lines and short phrases are mixed or isolated; the left-hand side no longer pulls the words towards it like gravity. When you see the page as Eigner did it brings natural comparisons with a canvas, a frame of sight, but also a container, a mind, a body in itself. Jennifer Bartlett, a scholar of Eigner's work, says his use of words on the page created "cognitive maps of his internally distanced relation to space." I'm deeply attracted to the possibilities inherent in this; it is an approach that anyone who has a body can utilise, especially the disabled, those whose body-minds exist in different ways. In building my voice I've been influenced heavily by Eigner to change the way I use form, moving the couplets to the page's right-hand side, and utilising single lines in space to exaggerate their syntactical impact:

we bury ourselves like readers in books
    take each other apart

        & put each other back again & again

            cripples love best
        because love is an assembly

                & we have always been broken

By using the breadth of the page, on one level there is an implicit resistance to the tradition of stanzaic blocks (indented to the left) as used by the majority of abled writers. In contrast, and inspired by Eigner, my poem 'flies' across the page, with word groupings and phrases staggered and 'mid-air' like the flocks of birds I can see from my window. It's no coincidence that my next collection is called *single window* – one pane of glass is the main point of contact between myself and the outside world, as I spend a large amount of my time housebound. Eigner's poems contained various observations, and half-trails of thought seen from his window, as if life outside were entering through his eyes, and out of the finger and thumb he used at the typewriter. I've been inspired by Eigner to write about the contrast between my own life and that outside the window, which I see as a barrier, rather than a portal, reflecting the sparsity of options in our life indoors.

I briefly mentioned space earlier, and this is something I'm using in a different way now: to represent the absences around the disabled body, and the narratives I'm constructing, which are often punctuated by periods of fatigue, sleep and brain fog. In her paper 'Into the White', Sarah Juliet Lauro states that the space Eigner uses can "make blankness visible as an active significatory presence at work in the text" and it's this idea that interests me. By drawing attention to certain words surrounded by space, I can bring to the fore significant events that occur within the otherwise banal periods of time my wife and I spend in pain.

My third collection, *single window*, is all about things that happen in our household, and because of that I've been using photography as a tool to help focus on the objects that fill our day-to-day lives. In previous work, I have tended towards creating poems that build to some universal meaning. But to convey the banality of the life I lead at home, I needed to find new ways to focus closer on the smaller things, the everyday occurrences. So I turned to my iPhone, and curated pictures of tablets, pill packets, spilt morphine, dirty laundry, and the general ephemera that inhabits our world and is a direct result of our disabilities and the pain that limits what we can do. Doctors' appointments, hospital visits, and other medical events were also recorded through snapshots to document the journey our bodies must undertake, from one clinical setting to another.

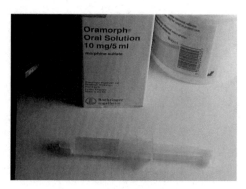

Above: oral morphine
Below: my wife having an immunosuppressant transfusion
(images: © Daniel & Emily Brenchi-Sluman)

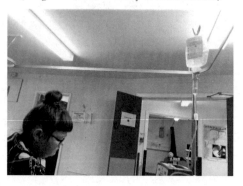

These pictures act like a filing system for the way my life moves from day to day, and they bring into sharp focus – for the reader – some of the things I take for granted, like the syringes of morphine, the b12 injections, and the ground-up CBD flowers to help insomnia. Whilst I am using some of them in my next collection, many have proved useful as triggers for new poems, and to enhance existing poems so they better reflect my life. The desire to make my voice hyper-confessional is both a personal and a political decision. The simple representation of disabled bodies and experiences, and the isolation many of us feel, is a strong political act – in a time when ableist narratives hold sway from tabloids to government policies. Apart from using pictures, I've been focusing on the worst parts of our day, when my wife and I are in serious pain, when we're recovering from surgery, or have been prescribed a medication that comes with unexpected side effects. I want my voice to sink into the unchartered crevices and holes of the disabled experience:

one of us is always appearing
to the other

in a scribbled haze of cigarette smoke

used pill-packets spread
like sunlight over the sofa

5mg of diazepam drifting
through my body like rain

in your hand
a bloody scrap of tissue

like a burst party balloon
as you fall asleep on the toilet

As I have been putting my experiences on the page, turning them in the light to find the best angles of approach, I have also been studying the work of poets who are othered in different ways, and how they have encoded their experiences through form and language. I found a wealth of queer and trans poets with corresponding poetics that gave me the excitement I needed to continue. Here were poems where the body was radically reimagined, where stigma was turned over in the poets' hands to show the insidious ways it moves through modern life, where arbitrary narratives about what is considered *normal* were flipped over so many times they fell apart in readers' minds. Although my own experiences of prejudice and barriers to access were different from many of these poets, we seemed to share a curiosity of the body-mind, and where it fits in with the rest of the world.

As I continue to write after my third book, I will accumulate new habits from further research, I will read the beautiful poems of others that will forever affect the way I write, and, as life changes me, the way I use the page will change to reflect this. The idea of altering our voice, refitting it, or even just maintaining our voice to ensure we are saying what we mean – with every tool at our disposal – is something I hope becomes discussed much more in poetry circles and academia. Every decision you make on the page (and there are thousands even in the simplest sonnet) represents who you are, what you believe in, and maybe even who you want to read your words.

✐ Writing Exercise

Using the camera on your phone (or any camera if your phone doesn't have one), catalogue your day as you move through it, paying particular attention to the ephemera, the detritus, the wake you leave behind – anything concrete. Having given yourself enough time to forget the specifics of these images, open them up on a day you have some time and write anything about them that catches your eye or feels especially tactile. It could be the way light glints off a coffee cup, the shape of your inhaler, or the beaten steel of the locker at the swimming pool you visit.

Rather than pure ekphrasis, use these images to explore the way you live, the habits you keep, and how they can be connected to broader aspects of who you are.

JANE COMMANE

Poetry and the Universe:
On the Art of Persisting

"A good poem is a contribution to reality. The world is never the same once a good poem has been added to it. A good poem helps to change the shape and significance of the universe"
– Dylan Thomas, *Poets on Poetry*, 1946.

I have written poetry in one form or another for almost as long as I have been able to write. It is a habit that has persisted throughout my life, an indelible part of who I am and how I receive and try to understand the world; it is part of my personal universe. As a child, I spent a lot of time in my own world – I had imaginary friends, and made tiny illustrated books of poems from the reams of dot-matrix paper my Dad brought home from work. I loved it when teachers at school asked us to write poetry, invariably making acrostic poems and enjoying the clever way the form worked, how a word generated something new entirely out of itself.

Poetry is a way of thinking, and a way paying attention; of language as accretion – words around ideas, gathering like lichen to a pebble. I often 'think' a poem long before I write it, sometimes for months or even years at a time. I like to 'live' with the ideas of poems. These I carry with me, little counterweights.

*

What happens if you throw your little pebble poem out, into space? If you're lucky enough, and there is water and gravity, it might land in a body of water that holds and swallows it whole, and you might see the ripples it has left behind, reaching the shore.

*

In the deepest days of lockdown in the winter of 2020-21, I found myself in zero gravity, caught in anxieties that I now realise I've lived with for most my life, but which the pandemic had brought sharply into focus. I began to imagine myself as an astronaut: home, a little capsule cast into fathomless space, shrinking smaller around me and those I love.

I found myself turning back to the things that have always sustained me: music, films, books, familiar voices that have long provided inspiration – the live source that brought me to poetry and writing in the first place.

As a youngster who found the loud, crowded and intimidating secondary school environment difficult, retreating back into music was my first place of sanctuary and belonging – but music (thanks to the Manic Street Preachers, whose album-sleeve quotes became something like a map out of my small-town teenage world) also brought me full circle to poetry and literature, encountering Sylvia Plath, Primo Levi, Philip Larkin and others. Later, Bloodaxe's *The New Poetry* anthology also tuned me into the especial way poetry can be comrade-companion – a reason to *persist* – and way to create a place, a community of words, to imaginatively reside and exist within. Even through times of not-writing, I have found the continued presence of poetry and that deep-rooted connection cognitively to language reassuring – reinforcing the power of creativity to give shape and significance to my own interior universe.

*

It could be said that the age of climate catastrophe and global pandemic is also one in which we might reassess and consider the use and relevance of poetry when we sit down to write – what use the human act of creation, of a poet making a poem, in the face of so much destruction and loss?

What use is even a 'good' poem? It can't oust bad governments, prevent war or illness, take carbon from the atmosphere and bury it back into the earth. The enormity of the problems we face, and our own inability to wield urgent change feels overwhelming. The words we may conjure onto a page may seem too slick or easy, or simply irrelevant.

I counter that poetry *can* do something small and elemental. If it can alter just an atom of perception or comprehension in our consciousness, then perhaps it can make possible a sense that change is possible in a collective, universal way.

If a poem can alter an atom of someone else's being – by forging connection through language, the sense that *yes, someone else knows this feeling too*, or *someone else knows just the exact shade of red of that sunset* or *I hadn't thought of that in this way before*, then a circuit is somehow complete. The lightbulb is lit and the charge is carried. A poem alters the shape of someone else's inner universe by tiny, irrevocable, amounts.

*

To write what might be thought of as a 'good' poem we have to be alive and observant of the world and of what it contains at a moment in time. A telescope trained into light years of space, able to adjust and see the infinitesimal detail and its part in infinity. A poet is, after all, someone who observes carefully – whether into themselves or out into the world, or indeed simultaneously into both, as some of our very best 'good' poems do.

A poem can be an act of being seen, of survival, hope, solidarity, a leap into the imagined 'otherspace' in parallel to that 'outerspace' we all live within. Poetry is the act of encountering impossibilities, and of imagining the possible as a way *towards* the making possible.

*

If we are to think about why we might want to continue to write and live with poems as part of us, here are reasons we might consider for the persistence of poetry:

Sensemaking

Writing a poem is a way of processing, thinking and trying to make sense of our experiences as living beings. Rather than reaching a solution or conclusion as an objective, a poem can be a way of reaching towards *something* – even if that something is ungraspable, just out of reach, our fingers tracing its form or its absence in space. Poetry is way of encountering uncertainties and, in the spirit of Keats' 'negative capability', poetry can be a space in which to hold multiplicities or multiple uncertainties or complexities, or even opposing things.

Namemaking

Poetry allows us to wield the power to name and to rename; to give voice, to take power back by naming for ourselves, or to give shape and form to those things which may otherwise elude us. To name and to describe in our own way is a vital assertion in a world that so quickly moves to erase, against unstoppable time and its ability to make of everything dust, against systems that would rather pretend you do not exist and render you powerless and voiceless.

Poetry as a form of knowing

Of attempting to know yourself, your fellow humans and human nature a little better. Of attempting to know the world about us and the living things at work within it a little better. Of possessing a kind of inquisitive knowledge that isn't about providing solutions or answers necessarily but is about the pursuit, encountering and experiences of imbibing of knowledge as curious, questioning beings. A position of openness, that in turn opens poems to others as a shared place of experience, knowledge and encountering.

Poem as a Charm Against Loss

The read-only memory of a poem; where we attempt to save things from irretrievable loss. The poem acts as a place to store, document, witness and protect against the limits of time – a space where something can be restored, conjured, called back to life from extinction within the poems' confines and exist also within the imagination of anyone who reads it. The preservation and passing on of the stories that made us.

Existing / Persisting

And to expand on that, poetry as an act of perseverance and persistence in the face of all these things; an act of faith. It says: *I was here, I have lived in this world, and this is my voice. I leave this behind that it may be heard, felt, known, and acknowledged, that I persisted and existed amongst you and we have shared this kind of stranger's communion through language in the moment of reading this poem.* Legacy – and communion with a greater universe we will never fully meet.

A tribute to the source

We write as part of a continuum of ideas. Always one leading to another and another. We might write to honour or pay tribute or as a reaction to or from the source materials that first inspired us to write. Our own writing might also one day be another's spark, shape another's understanding of the universe – or it will join the rest of the undiscovered space matter, waiting for an eye at the telescope.

A space for imaginary possibility

The power of creating other alternate realities; to acknowledge there are other ways to exist; to acknowledge the problems of our existing realities. That things don't have to be how they are. That the imagination allows and affords us this is transformative, radical, enlivening – and sustaining in frightening, dark times. Alternate realities enable us see the existing one aslant and all the more clearly for its errors. It isn't escapism to use our imaginations to their fullest extent, or to acknowledge that humans could, if they chose to, create a heaven for each other on the earth.

*

The universe reminds us that it is vast. There are endless possibilities, endless possible galaxies that we will never have time to explore. That we are very small, a mere scrape on time, amidst all of this.

Hurry, whispers the universe. The depths of imagination are boundless, but we only have the here and now, this spark in the darkness, to explore them.

*

In releasing our poems, and in engaging with being published and public, we encounter gravitational forces on our work that are outside of the creative realm. The pressure to compete with our peers, to enter and put our work before systems that judge it, to compete for funding or employment or commissions. All of which may bring to bear on the poet all kinds of expectations, some of which can be useful, or used to motivate and fuel our work, but which also may not always be creative, productive or positive pressures. Mixed blessings.

The question of how to manage this force, rather than it managing *you* is important to our creative health and the openness and generosity with which we write at our best. Poets, like all writers, are bound in that strange orbit that requires both that we must create alone in private, yet desire also to find a public audience for what we have made, without the latter impinging on the imaginative universes of the former.

*

If poetry is a part of who we are, there is also a distinct danger in yoking a part of your own selfhood to the success,

107

or otherwise, of your creative work. At worst, it can be utterly destructive of creative abilities, a feedback loop that consumes the original joy of writing and participating in poetry.

Everything about the poetry and publishing industry seems finite; prizes, money, publication, likes and limelight. Only so much of it can exist. Sometimes it can seem that no matter how hard we have tried, a 'good' poem is sent out on its voyage and we wait for it to send back its little pings of connection data, only for it to report back nothing, silence in its wake.

Perhaps a poet might stop writing altogether, or find the poems they write aim to succeed in certain arenas but end up trailing in the bright wake of other's comet-tail of success. The stratosphere seems to have little oxygen and can be an oppressive environment in which to try and create good things.

If it makes persevering with our own creativity seem pointless, that's at least in part because the value system of the creative industries, and of all marketplaces in the end, entail a very different value system to that which fuels creativity in the first place. The commercial, capitalist world by which books and brands are sold, when mapped directly over a creative one, creates forcefields of status, success, targets and pressures to achieve certain material objectives which have little to do with the motivations we may have set out with when starting to write.

The poets who best manage to keep these centripetal forces in check acknowledge the parts of the system it is useful to engage with, but take care to keep this from intruding on the sacred space of creating and writing. They keep their ideas about poems and the aims they have for what poetry might achieve at arm's length from the aims that the industries and marketplaces may have in mind for whatever they create in the end. There is a protective forcefield around their writing desks, a lead-lined room that rebounds false signals.

They also find ways to put their skills to good use. Many are teachers, mentors and encouragers, who understand the value of sharing knowledge, genuinely and generously. They open doors for other writers, give wholeheartedly back to the poetry universe.

They acknowledge that disappointments and failures are part of a writer's lot at times, and they try to keep things magnanimous; the vortex of rivalries and envy held in check. Even in periods where their own creativity is fallow, the energy they give out remains – and is a sustaining force.

The first law of thermodynamics: *energy cannot be created, nor can it be destroyed; energy can only be transferred, or changed from one form to another*. So it goes with creative energies too.

This way of tapping into the energy of a creative life on its own terms seems to me to be a good way to protect both our creativity and our mental wellbeing as writers, ensuring a long, positive relationship with the 'craftform' as well as artform of poetry, and its myriad opportunities for fantastic voyaging, no matter what the trajectory.

*

You may turn your papers over and begin: a fast, frantic scribbler in exams, I was desperate to get everything out of my head and onto the paper. Blue biro'd fingers, aching. That summer of GCSEs stretches long and hot in the dusty assembly hall that smelt of varnish, trainers and crisps. I was furiously trying to write my way out, a passport for something else beyond, to a galaxy of books and poems and music and imagination and ideas, desperate to reach it, wherever it was.

Here we all are, scribbling, racing against the clock to get it down on to paper.

*

It's urgent. Poetry, I mean, the urge to make it; I know when I need to write. And I know too when my little capsule needs to return to base-camp for the supplies that replenish and keep me travelling on. Trust in the trajectory. Out into inner space. *Ping. Ping. Ping.*

*

Come down. Tell me, what's the view like from the furthest edge of your universe?

✐ Writing Exercise

Write a poem by returning to the 'original source' of your own inspiration as a writer. What was it that first made you want to write poems? What was your *Big Bang* moment?

It might be another poem that you first encountered at the start of your earliest experiences as a poet. But it doesn't have to be: it could be a film, a piece of music, a book or an artwork that was part of your own awakening as an artist – something elemental, which inspires or moves you. In making this piece of art, the creator moved something in you – altered the 'shape or significance' of *your* personal universe.

Return to this and immerse yourself. Make notes, explore this piece of art and respond to it wholeheartedly with all of your own reactions, emotions and sensory responses. Don't worry at this point about making a poem. Observe and be open to the whole-body experience of being in the moment with this artwork and write down everything you notice, however small.

Return to your notes in a few days and start redrafting, allow what you write (or rewrite) to be intuitive – tune in to the form or shape it may be taking and allow the source material you've created to inform its own direction. See if you can sense the line breaks and formal choices the work suggests it needs and allow instinct to lead your creative choices.

VAHNI CAPILDEO

Skull Sutra:
On Writing the Body

Body of the Text: Decade of Beginning
String together ten ways to write the body. This will help you lose count.

If you don't have any way of recording your writing, write in your head. This is a skull sutra. If you don't like the look of Mother Kali dancing, that is because Truth arrives blackly, already burnt. The skulls around her neck are all of us when we aren't in a position to put on a face.

If the eyes of the painting follow you around the room, and the wardrobe, when you open it, is full of beautiful feminine clothing, you are in the past. You are my parents who arrived at the town in France with nowhere to stay and were offered a flat inhabited by a portrait. Like them, you flee to the station and ask for *un billet pour n'importe où*. Ticket to wherever.

Wherever is your body? Write the environment right up to where your body is. Your body will jellyfish, tendrilling into voluminous, negative space. How does the environment change as you place the borders for what it is, what is not-you?

If the eyes of the painting are closed, know that you are perfectly, lovingly beheld.

Does your body figure in distant people's interiority?

Beads, seeds, resin, wood, pearl, ceramic, glass, come at a price. You have a skull. Wear it like a necklace of at least ten skulls.

If I were you, I would move carefully.

If I were you, I would pay more attention to the string.

That is the absolute opposite of what you are doing.

Why Hasn't She Found Her Voice: Decade of Not Looking for It
I wrote poetry under the illusion that poetry could be a form of drama.

I wrote poetry in ignorance of the role of poet as performer.

I collected voices and believed that so long as they remained on the page, they would rise off the page, limitless, unlike their author.

Voices passed through me. No voice inhabited me. No voice could rule me.

Grey clouds in the sky gained blue and purple depth. The wind gained a voice. For years, I could not differentiate the voice of the wind from the turbulence in the trees. Then I heard it, awful as wolves, coming over the foothills of the northern range. I ran around the house to hear it and learnt to write a voice that always is arriving, affecting the land without itself landing, a voice whose force has no body.

I read in the newspapers about the Soviet boy who allegedly stopped growing but tricked his body into starting to grow again by eating tomato sandwiches. I read a comic book about Wonder Woman playing 'bullets and bracelets' on a Greek island and riding a horse. For a while I lived on tomato sandwiches in order to grow six feet tall and learnt in detail about how to care for a horse I never would own. I cleaned the frog of its hooves tenderly. At the age of sixteen I started writing poems again, after a five-year break during which my piano was my horse. I had grown to five feet two and a half inches. I wrote poems in the voice of a long-dead and heroic man, and perhaps his horse. They were my body.

I wrote poetry when I began to hear absurdities sailing from between the lips of comfortable bodies. I bodied the absurdities in verse to amp them up and put them on replay. I felt sure that those words moved about in a bulk of soft cloth with hard seams: well-worn trousers and jackets.

I wrote poetry believing that we were looking at the same page, not that you would look for me in the page.

I wrote as if we were sharing the book, side-by-side.

More voices and more bodies arrived on the page, in narrow-gauge poems, drainpipe poems, bridge poems, cigarette poems, one-way-street poems. So long as nobody lingered too long, they all fit. The moment in the city was the central character. Did I confuse you? You like the playhouse too.

Bodies Unsaid, Bodies Understood: Decade of the Figures in the Margin

When do occurrences from biographical reality tend towards prose genres, not poetry?

The murdered bodies. Where would I put the murdered bodies – whose thighs, burnt with an iron; whose head, smashed with a toilet lid; whose head, with a hat and sunglasses placed on it – are not mine to mourn, or yours to gawp at?

What kind of crime novel would that make? Does it do for a villanelle?

The gorgeous bodies. Where would the gorgeous bodies play – the Rastafarian jumping off his boat to dance, knees lifting high, in the surf; the woman in the full-body integrity of deep gyration, innocent-faced, wearing only a tiny gold shield over her pubic mound; the Jamaican guest back at dawn from the opening of Trinidad's Carnival, washing blue paint off his body with a green hosepipe and reaching for a scarlet towel draped on the branch of a tree?

What kind of romance novel would that make? Do I owe them each their own ode?

The doctor bodies. Where would I put the British doctor who laughed in my viral face and sent me away, dehydrated, to fall, concussed, behind a locked door in a rented room; the other British doctor who told my agonised father in his fifties that he should go down the stairs on his bottom from now on; the Trinidad doctor who removed the cyst pressing on a nerve in my father's spine, so that he left walking upright, released?

What kind of misery memoir would that make? Does it argue for the shine of a sonnet sequence?

The avoided bodies. Where would my answer be to your email when you asked how I (really) was, "apart from the exotica"? What would my answer be to my answer, when I thanked you for asking about my avoidance of my (real) self; how would I convey my disturbance at the everyday communicating itself as exotica; how could you receive my ecological sense of my real self as environmental, meaningfully dispersed?

What kind of mind-body-spirit manual would that make? Is there any such thing as a truly open field, in poetry or on earth?

Haven't I already put some of these bodies, several times over, elsewhere –

Writing the Body: Decade of Identifying the Body
Become the student of your body. Sign up online to be schooled in mythologising your body. The flap of a crow on a northern skylight, the sight of your retroverted uterus on a screen, and the ache under your right ribs are the main locators – years apart – that your anxiously scanning brain finds for 'body'.

Disallow memory. Concentrate on sensation. Your left ribs are pain-free; much of your body is effectively non-existent.

Embrace memory. What is your earliest memory – your worst memory – your best memory? Remember delivering the creative writing session scripted by someone else. You had to ask these questions. Reluctance was your eyes. Apprehension was your ears. Intrusive was your name. The London undergraduates, normally a collection of individuals, stirred like one disturbed amoeba. The most generous undergraduate snapped off from the collective discomfort. She ran, weeping, into the corridor.

Worst memories are delivered regularly. You have a back catalogue. Best memories used to take the form of highlights. Now they are the times when the least happens.

Consider the celebration of the body in proper rhetorical order, from the radiance of the crown of the head, point by point, down to the smallest toe. Describe yourself as if you were a queen. To be radiant, you decompose into a composite body. Memory appears to be the ruler of your body. Your hair is your grandmother's, diademed with Indian wedding jewellery you have seen only in a photograph. Your eyes are the paintbrush of astigmatism, glorifying everything that has an edge into the ambiguity of glowing curve. Your body appears to be a tent supporting an inherited sequence of traits becoming face. Elbows? Stomach? Must try harder. Your toes, your toes collide with things, your toes are mini-disasters.

Write a perfect body in proper rhetorical order, and step into it. Nobody notices what you wear, anyway.

They give you strange language for how to experience your body. Heavy your leg; heavy it into the floor. Let your internal organs sink. Draw the figure of eight with your pelvis. Dance outside your feet. Float your bones. Take your skeleton for a swim. Open your mouth! Catch flies!

Body is a compounding word. Bodywork. Body-mind.

They expect the language they give you not to be strange. Intramuscular. Angiogram. Stent. Stent. Catheterise. Intubate. General. Local.

It takes a team of people to put the body to sleep and wake it up again. Stay awake this time. Look, it's doing what it should. Your insides are on-screen.

Taking a Line for a Walk: Decade of Actual, Literal Walks
And even if I did not refer to it, the poem would have the feel of the walk having happened. How beautiful your feet running disembodied through the former internment camp for Germans and German Jews, now a tropical garden in the residential neighbourhood. How beautiful your feet running as a second pair alongside my bare, brown ones, during the school holidays, along the hot concrete walkway surrounding a private house. How beautiful your unreconstructable feet.

I am walking with you in white, sprigged cotton. When you are doing the fire drill for the poem, you must count this among the poem's addressees.

And even if I did not refer to it, the poem would have the feel of the walk having happened. How jagged your path as you walk through lines of traffic, directing traffic. How jagged your path as you gesture gracefully, a mental policeman in the uniform of a vagrant. How jagged the enjambments of pavement and road in your path.

I am walking with you in a scavenged jacket. When you are doing the census for the poem, you must count this among the poem's employed.

And even if I did not refer to it, the poem would have the feel of the walk having happened. How rounded your posture as you turned your back on your bus, missed it deliberately, and asked a question of a man with terrified eyes. How rounded your posture as you said kindly to the man with terrified eyes, "Come. Come." How rounded your posture as you walked with him while he walked as if walking alone.

I am walking with you in bystander polyester. When you are doing the costs for the poem, you must not discount this, because it was full price.

And even if I did not refer to it, the poem would have the feel of the walk having happened. How determined your stride as the three of you walk down the pavement, dressed up for a night out, your eyes fixed on anticipated pleasure. How determined your stride as the three of you walk into me, so I collapse into a shop window, dropping my phone, which shatters, and one of you sees me. How determined your stride as the one of you who sees me pauses, asks "Are you okay?" How shocked that one looks when I say *no*, how you continue.

I am walking with you in what doubles as office wear and exercise gear. When you are working out the destination of the poem, you might count this as destination unknown.

And even if I did not refer to it, the poem would have the feel of the walk having happened. How divergent your stride from the gravelled line as you stare at me with an unspeaking smile, crossing the green blank between the new development and the main road. How divergent your stride as you narrow the space into which I am walking, and you carry your wife with you, widening the barrier. How divergent your stride as you grin without a word and I am walked off the gravel into the green blank, which is muddy.

I am walking with you in the guise of a detestable pronoun. Do not detest too much.

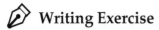 **Writing Exercise**

Arrange ten objects, or have someone arrange them for you, in one place, if you live in one place. For example: stones; pieces of waste paper; perfume samples; fancy knots or clumps of thread or wool; seeds or pips or beads. If you do not live in one place, collect objects that you can easily travel with and discard, such as waste paper; or write a list of ten real objects that you know well, though you are not carrying them with you.

Take ten units of time, not too far from each other. This might be ten days within one month, or ten days one after another, or ten continuous hours, or a minute now and then.

In each unit of time, stay with the object. Handle it if you can. Hold it in your thoughts if you do not have it with you. Tell it "I am" as if you are saying "I love you".

Towards the end of each unit of time, make a written, typed or recorded note of any bodily awareness, change in bodily state, bodily distractions, or memories of bodily experiences that occurred while you were concentrating on the object. This should give you ten notes about yourself. Pick one word from each.

Gather the objects up, placing them close together to make a shape, or throw them away carefully. The ten words are your prompts. Use them to string together a way of telling the body; for example, grow a line around each word, or place them at the beginning or end of a line.

SARAH CORBETT

The Long Game:
On Making a Life in Poetry

I never intended to write poetry. Growing up I wanted to be
a farmer, a spy, a journalist (specifically Kate Adie, who was
on the TV a lot in the seventies and eighties), a horse vet, a
riding instructor (I remain a qualified riding instructor), then
an artist. If I was going to write, then it would be fiction. Poets,
I learnt at school, were male, and too close to the gods for me to
ever come near them. It wasn't until I read the poetry of Carol
Anne Duffy, Vicky Feaver, Penelope Shuttle, Sharon Olds, did
I think, *I can do this, I can take my place amongst these poets.*

From an early age I wrote stories and illustrated them, made
them into little books, until I was about fourteen and boys (and
more illicit things) took my attention. When I did start writing,
at university in Leeds, I wrote stories – or tried to – until a light
that followed me around for six months after a breakdown
in my first year entered my head, and I wrote my first poem.
I believe the poem was released by the breakdown, and the
continued writing enabled by the care I received from Leeds
University's Mental Health Service; I owe them my writing and
my life. I published my first poems a year after that. Writing
poetry was more thrilling than riding horses or taking drugs
because it came from inside of me, wasn't reliant on anything
other than this communion, and I was spellbound; I knew I'd
found the thing I would spend the rest of my life pursuing.
I had found my vocation, or perhaps more accurately, it had
found me.

I realised, in the few years that followed, that poetry had been
seeking me out since I was very young. As soon as I could talk,
I was singing; as soon as I was singing, I was making up songs.

As soon as I could read, I was trying to decipher the books on my father's bookshelves. Amongst the art books and sets of classics in their red and green covers, there were poetry books – Shakespeare's sonnets and Keats' collected poems, as well as *The Oxford Book of Twentieth Century English Verse* edited by Philip Larkin, I still have. I vividly recall, at about five years old, trying to read Keats' poems, their strange charm, arcane and impenetrable but mesmerising, magical.

Then at secondary school in North Wales I was introduced to Dylan Thomas and Gerard Manly Hopkins, two poets who had a profound effect on me. The visionary lyricism of *Under Milk Wood*, which we listened to as a class and then read out, and Hopkins' extraordinary cadences, spoke to the unexpressed musician-mystic in me. As the teacher read the lines "World broods with warm breast and with ah! bright wings", from Hopkins's poem 'God's Grandeur', I left my body and hovered at the back of the class – an ecstatic experience. What I thought poetry was and should be was fixed in me then.

After two years travelling and teaching English, I got down to the business of trying to become a poet, endlessly practising forms and metre, writing mostly rubbish until I started writing about my mother, who had left when I was four years old; a major breakthrough, these poems formed the backbone of my first collection. The next breakthrough came when I attended a course at the Arvon Foundation at Lumb Bank in West Yorkshire. Here I met Susan Wicks, who said *you have to do this*, and pointed me in the direction of awards and courses. I won an Eric Gregory award in 1997, and *The Red Wardrobe* was published by Seren Books in 1998, and shortlisted for the Forward Best First Collection Prize and the T. S. Eliot Prize (almost unheard of then for a debut). I had a fabulous time being invited to festivals and giving readings, being interviewed for newspapers, my work widely reviewed and applauded.

And then my father died, I had a baby (born the night of the readings for the T. S. Eliot Prize), realised too late that I was in a disastrous marriage, and headed towards a period of severe depression, financial distress and immense personal struggle that took more than ten years to climb out of. I published two further collections with Seren Books, *The Witch Bag* in 2002, centred around motherhood and the death of my father, and *Other Beasts* (2008). The reception of *The Witch Bag* was devastating. I hadn't realised it, but women poets were not meant to write about miscarriage, abortion, childbirth, periods, sexual desire, grief, and certainly not with such candour. The freedom to write honestly and openly of the female lived experience is one of the most significant changes in British poetry in recent years, as well as the proliferation of women poets on publishers' and prize lists; but it is a relatively recent development. Ironically, it was a female critic who lamented how the poems in *The Witch Bag* focused on women's experience, and not on the *human* experience.

I didn't write another word for three years. The lively public and critical interest in my work ceased – I'm still not sure why – and, with the battles I was fighting (single motherhood, mental illness, isolation and poverty), I retreated. These were the years of 9/11 and the wars that followed that seemed to herald the end of times, although in fact they were the beginning of a new period of historical upheaval and social change, with a greater threat about to become clear: climate change. But Seren were encouraging – wasn't it time for a third collection? A course at The Poetry Business, then based in Huddersfield, set me back on my writing feet. My third collection, *Other Beasts*, felt very much torn, slowly and painfully, out of this long silence, and it met, mostly, with silence. I knew I had lost something essential to a successful poetry career. I'd lost touch with the environment of poetry which was rapidly changing, expanding and diversifying, and never quite got to grips with the social media revolution. I might write explicitly and candidly in my poetry, but this was experience transformed by art and I had no interest in sharing my private life in public. Something, I felt, had to be preserved. The only result was anonymity, my very own invisibility cloak.

I think in part the backlash against my second collection was to do with the then pervasive negative ideas around female 'confessional' writing, in particular the writing of poets such as Sylvia Plath and Anne Sexton, who are strong influences on my work. I first came across Plath's poetry during my A levels, although at the time I didn't know that the poems which moved me so powerfully, 'Mushrooms' and 'Elm', were by her, or even by a female poet. I had an inspired (male) English teacher who would give us poems outside the syllabus to read, omitting the names of the poets so we would focus entirely on the poem. That teacher used to call me 'the bard' but when asked why would say, *you'll find out one day.* I was discovering an unusual facility for responding to poetry, and whilst I had no idea about writing poetry, he clearly saw that one day I would get this idea and follow it. When I finally discovered Plath's work for myself, it spoke in its pain and complexity and stark, uncompromising beauty so deeply of my own life and artistic passions that it became the supreme standard, for me, of the art form. Above all, Plath's poetry gave me permission to write directly about my own mental suffering, but also the embodied experience of womanhood.

I moved to Pavilion Poetry in 2015, the new imprint at Liverpool University Press. Pavilion published my verse novel, *And She Was*, which experiments with voice and story and form and points to my enduring interest in narrative, and, in 2018, *A Perfect Mirror*. I'm now working on a new book due to be published, tentatively, in 2023. A conversation with my editor, Deryn Rees-Jones, that began with *let's schedule in your next book,* was certainly the catalyst to focusing this time around. Despite my thirty years of working with poetry, beginning this new book feels terrifying, until I start in earnest and the energy of the poem takes hold. As you get older, every new book, every new poem can feel like this; it's one of the hazards of a long career. My fifth collection, *A Perfect Mirror*, opens with the phrase "I am new to this", because that's how it feels, every time.

There's a pattern to a writing life that can only be viewed in retrospect: the importance of teachers who listen to their instincts and encourage you to listen to yours, more experienced poets who point you in the right direction, editors who support and care for your work and the longevity of that endeavour. There were times, without these poets and editors and teachers, many of them friends, when I might have given up. Writing poetry can be a lonely business, but the life of poetry can be full of adventure and friendship and fun; hold out for those times, I tell myself. More importantly, fight your way back to that spell, that moment of enchantment when a poem is born – and then, as Heaney says, "Cultivate a work-lust".

During lockdown, and especially in winter when my small house can feel like a prison, I'm experimenting with writing in my son's room whilst he's away at university. The room looks out to Heptonstall, and the spire of the new church behind which Sylvia Plath is buried. Plath's poetry remains, like a shaman's "rattle-bag", a source of power whenever I return to it, although the muses of my new book are the Russian and European poets of the mid twentieth-century. Even when you're alone with your writing you are never entirely alone; the long river of poetry that extends into the past and into the future is always within reach. This is also part of the pattern. There's another part too, just as important, of life itself, how it interrupts, takes over, knocks you off course. But if I stray too far, the poetry pulls me back – through dreams mostly, or a kind of health in my body; I think poetry has been so much a part of making me, of keeping me sane and healthy and alive, that it's knitted into my bones.

Plath taught me to look into the dark despite the fear, and to find an answer to it; she also taught me staying power, discipline, and the belief that poetry is centrally important to the artistic, intellectual and spiritual life of a culture. Even though I no longer have the tremendous energy I had in my twenties that Plath also had, it's this central belief that keeps me coming back to poetry, even when it lets me down – along with the sense that poetry is a gift, and the vocation of poetry needs to be honoured. In many ways it gets harder – parenting, teaching, other writing stealing time and focus, the loss of something youth gives you: energy, certainty, that courage anyway – and in other ways it gets easier: the sense of work achieved, letting go of unrealistic expectations (but never of hope), a publisher committed to my work, and an editor who encourages risk and experimentation.

Why do I write poetry? Because it's part of me, and connects me to something bigger, more magnificent than myself. If I had to give advice, I'd say write for the joy of it, but look after your work in the world. Have a plan, but be prepared to have those plans diverted; be prepared for failure. Keep faith with the art of poetry – of craft, experiment and play. Always be on to the next thing, and the next; the future is an endless possibility. Who knows what you will create?

✎ Writing Exercise

Invent your own poetry form

We're all familiar with traditional poetry forms (or should be!) – the sonnet, the sestina, the ghazal, the villanelle, to name a few – but these forms started somewhere, with ideas and invention developed to fit a purpose, and were then taken up and practised by generations of poets until they became a tradition. Imported forms have also always been adapted: think of how the Elizabethans – Wyatt, and then Shakespeare – took the Italian sonnet (little song) and made it simpler, to suit English rhyme and cadence. Contemporary poets have invented forms too: there's the 'specular', created by Julia Copus, with the second half of the poem reflecting the first.

How might you go about inventing your own form? The first thing you need to do is to set some rules. A poetry form must place *specific pressure* on the language of the poem, make demands of line and metre or syllabic count, shape and length, stanza form and rhyme; it must create a *frame for expression*. Think about what the form is for – many forms were originally designed as expressions of love, or religious thought, such as George Herbert's shape poem 'Easter Wings'. You might consider building something personal into the form. If it is your thirtieth year, for example, might you have ten stanzas of three lines, include a message or a name, just as a ghazal must include the name of the poet? Whatever you create may not get passed on down the ages, but it will teach you about the importance of form, and how each element of the poem's shape and structure is an integral part of its expression. Hopefully, you'll also have fun as you work, because writing poetry should be joyful work, one of the integral rewards of writing poetry that can sustain you for a lifetime.

JO CLEMENT

Poetry as Patrìn:
On Writing Your Truth, Not Someone Else's

For centuries, Gypsy, Roma and Traveller folk have crafted *patrìn*. This Romanes word expresses an assemblage of foliage that is gathered or twisted together. Handfuls of grass are swaddled, woven with bark strips, and then returned to the landscape. Placed in fields or by roadside hedges, *patrìn* quietly announce a diasporic presence in Britain. Families living on the road leave these discreet markers to tell others like us: *We slept here. It's safe.* To those fluent in this leaf language, these messages can transform a place into a page. Until they biodegrade, *patrìn* remind those who move along the ever-changing margins of ancient paths that we are still here.

Absence defines Gypsy, Roma and Traveller people as much as our presence. Encampments appear, then our wheeled and hooved homes move – or are moved – on. Historically, we were not obligated to conform to the official paperwork a settled identity demands. Birth or death certificates, house or land ownership, employment contracts or other documentation were impractical and irrelevant processes for a life on the move. Off paper, family histories, songs and stories continue to be passed down the generations in the oral tradition. Many of these ephemeral narratives and lyrics have been lost to time; others transform and survive.

As the poet David Morley said, "One of the reasons there isn't a huge amount of written Gypsy history is because Gypsies are hyper-aware of the dangers of writing things down and leaving signs." Our elders frowned upon writing because they knew these dangers first-hand.

Writing this essay is an act of disclosure because sharing my race continues to feel risky. Whether on the page or over coffee with a new friend, country people[1] might see me differently or make assumptions about my character and capacity, beliefs far worse than those I, raised in the Catholic tradition of shame, already carry. From childhood, I wrote secretly. First in chalk under tables, then in notebooks. If I were to become anything, let alone the writer I aspired to be, I couldn't afford to make this part of me known. In my imagination, I best understood my voice as *patrìn*, a tightly bound tongue. Truths as vulnerable as petals: hidden in plain sight.

To be a Gypsy, Roma and Traveller has been – and continues to be – a dangerous endeavour. In sixteenth-century Scotland we were invited to dance in royal courts and had decrees to roam freely awarded. We were also sentenced to expulsion or death, threatened with imprisonment, and were made to cease free movement altogether. Carrying the shame of our fabled forefather Cain, the punishment for being *found a Gypsy* was pillory, incarceration or banishment. Those who survived bore the physical and emotional scars of "mutilation … practised up till the beginning of the eighteenth century" (David MacRitchie, 'Scottish Gypsies Under the Stewarts', *Journal of the Gypsy Lore Society*). England, too, branded us a lower order, the letter *V* seared in our cheeks with hot irons to signify the 'Statute of Vagabonds' instituted by King Edward VI. A single letter became a communicative tool to pronounce us *others*. The English language was a weapon to be feared, so to survive we spoke our own tongues – variations of Cant, Jib and Romanes – and, wherever possible, we kept our identity silent.

When the Equality Act 2010 first legally acknowledged Traveller ethnicity, the binds of that silence, for me, began to loosen. I was in my mid-twenties and wrote poems that had developed the keen sense of metaphor that silencing

1. Non-Gypsy, Roma and Travellers who lead settled lives. Note: due to a historical lack of safe and legal site provision, many Gypsy, Roma and Traveller peoples now live in permanent housing or vacillate between the two modes.

and oppression necessitates. The bed-sheet dens I described were the tents and *vardos*[2] that my family once found shelter in. Ponies born in edgeland fields inked in biro were my ancestors; the words were silvered in caul and misty with hot blood. In one poem, I tentatively placed warm and feathered eggs in baskets, their shells as fragile as a bitten tongue, a slipped truth. From wood engravings to fireside songs, our culture and traditions shaped the figurative and sonic landscapes of my poems. I glossed the margins of my pages with Romanes and their translations into English. *Porajmos.*[3] *Phral.*[4] *Patrìn.* Writing was, for me, an act of defiance. Fuelled by anger toward institutional racism, I greeted each page like a stopping place. In my finest cursive, I found myself writing my great-grandma's name repeatedly: *Venus Smith.*

No photographs survive of Venus, and yet, on a landmark page, she emerged in a poem as pearl-like as Botticelli's goddess, her namesake. Venus remains one of the addressees to whom my poems speak. She first appeared in 'Caulbearer' on the periphery of a sequence of poems:

> When I followed Venus's
> wet skirt back into the water,
> it wrapped around me
> like the caul she bore
> my granda in
> and breathed:
>
> *We of the black curl*
> *bear these tides.*
> *We swallow pearls.*
> *We swallow time.*

---

2. A traditional wheeled horse-drawn Traveller's wagon painted and highly ornamented both inside and out with often gilded wood carvings. Also called a "living wagon".
3. Romani genocide (1939–45). The Holocaust Memorial Day Trust confirms that in World War Two 200,000 Roma and Sinti Travellers – 25% of the population – were killed.
4. Brother.

Time keeps me from ever meeting this incredible woman who was born and died on the road. But in a poem, a dialogue can flourish. The words of the great Robert Pinsky, in his 'Poem of Disconnected Parts' in *Gulf Music,* here reverberate loudly: "we do not / Worship our ancestors: we consult them." Venus, alive in the elegiac mode, speaks back.

Creative writing handbooks and workshops I have encountered over the years often ask writers to imagine themselves in one of many rooms within their homes. From Italian, *stanze* translates as "rooms", but I found it challenging to imagine my stanzas in this way. Don Paterson proposes poems can explore "a finite series of rooms [that] can then be furnished appropriately". W. N. Herbert terms this the "notion of the poem as house", a metaphor tailored to an interior way of understanding the world around us. Writing practice discourse has a substantial stake in this paradigm. Mary Oliver suggests poems are "well-made thing[s]" that require an architectural "sense of orderliness". Would my poems not be *"made well"* without a permanent imagined home to ground them? In Peter Sansom's exercise 'The Living Room', for instance, he invites poets to "imagine they are in their hallway or kitchen" and to walk toward their living room and reach for the door handle. A list of prompts is provided to then "furnish" the room. *Scaffolding* was a word that regularly accompanied almost all descriptions of the poetic craft I read and heard. All I could imagine were the temporary poles and planks Gypsy, Roma and Traveller builders might use to fix the roof of a settled home before they hopped back on the road and off to the next stopping place.

When writing toolkits prioritise dwelling culture, they assume the lens belonging to the white, settled majority and demonstrate the "unequal power relationships"[5] that Gypsy, Roma and Traveller people experience in their everyday lives.

5. Sergei Shubin and Kate Swanson, '"I'm an imaginary figure": Unravelling the mobility and marginalisation of Scottish Gypsy Travellers', *Geoforum*, 41/6 (November 2010), 919.

Being "an under-represented community" is symptomatic of our exclusion from "mainstream education systems".[6] A distrust of language and those in power who use it to oppress and demonise had led to silence. As David Morley says: "The danger is you disappear yourselves". I looked for my kin at university, in libraries and bookshops: I could not find us. We were nowhere and everywhere at once. I wanted my poems to acknowledge that absent presence and bring our history and my perspective to the page. The green bow-top *vardo*, an iconic Gypsy, Roma and Traveller home, emerged:

> Sure as the colts
> will nag the fillies,
> our living wagon
>
> prints itself
> across my mind.
> Lacquered
>
> like spring woods
> where it 'atches
> a spell,
>
> it's all cut
> in bonny birds
> and brushed
>
> with roses,
> windows laced

Unlike a house, the *vardo* is not defined by its interiority and obedience. Its presence in the landscape symbolises a dislocation from mainstream culture. At a time when Gypsy, Roma and Travellers faced shortages of legal stopping places, my stanzas ached for freedom of movement and identity:

---

6. Kalwant Bhopal, 'Gypsy Travellers and Education: Changing Needs and Changing Perceptions', *British Journal of Educational Studies*.

A wheel-bird
sent up
from its scrape

turns like silver
in pockets or my head
in this flat,

tight as bow-top
tarp static as pike
skin on flame.

I had begun to write against the idea of the poem-as-house. Why not think of the stanza differently? Stanzaic rooms serve and privilege the 'settled' imagination rather than a peripatetic or 'moveable' imagination, such as mine. *Stanza* can also mean 'station' or 'stopping-place' in Italian. End-stopped stanzas are suited to this translation because their punctuation signals a "grammatical boundary or break".[7] In musical notation, this silence is called a rest or caesura, it is a breath between musical phrases. A conductor decides the length of this breath in a concert. In a poem, the reader decides the length of the pause in an end-stopped stanza. Enjambed stanzas, however, are designed to vault readers forward onto the next. They perform like a prolonged bird's-eye, the pause in musical notation, a powerful durational pull that at once holds and carries the reader. In turned stanzas, these through sounds carry the reader. But as in the volta of a sonnet, turned lines can also iterate a new musical expression or thought. Rainer Maria Rilke's experimentation with end-stopped form in *The Sonnets to Orpheus* bring this to life. His fourth sonnet's octave splits into quatrains and the sestet into tercets. All are end-stopped, save for the final tercet, which closes with an ellipsis: "And yet there are the breezes ... there are the spaces ..."

---

7. Poetry Foundation, 'End-stopped', www.poetryfoundation.org/learn/glossary-terms/end-stopped.

Staked in the cultural significance and territories of people and place, I imagine each of my poems to be a stopping place or *'atchin tan*.[8] These are the sites of temporary encampments: empty fields, leafy roadside spots Gypsy, Roma and Traveller people pull in, loosen our braces, light a fire, and put the kettle on. They are the places that we draw on the handbrake and leave *patrìn*, before we move (or are moved) onto the next. Stopping, then, is a crucial part of the peripatetic passage in the same way silence – Rilke's breezy spaces – propels the music of a poem. By re-engaging with the stanza on my cultural terms, I ensure that the "emotional dimensions of mobility [are] not peripheral, but central"[9] to form. With this, I craft stanzas that are not vessels upon which meaning or cultural concerns are conferred but, rather, through the engine of musical form and imaginative compulsion, can reveal them.

Writing poetry is, for me, like making *patrìn:* the craft is itself integral to the message. By placing my literary art into the canon, I hope my poems can reach others, and, like *patrìn*, say: *I was here. I wrote this. It's safe.*

---

8. A contemporary version of the Romanes *achimasko tan*.
9. Shubin and Swanson, '"I'm an Imaginary Figure"'

Writing Exercise

I'd like you to imagine that you are alone inside a small tent. Let's lean into that for a few minutes. How does the light diffuse through the walls? What colour is it? How does the air smell or feel against your flesh? Write across your senses for a few minutes. If you get stuck, pick five words or short phrases to describe the way the ground beneath you feels.

Gently put your hand on the wall of the tent. There's a whole world beyond. What is happening out there? What can you discern? How? Write not just *what* you know but *how* you know it. Are you telling someone in particular? Pay attention to your addressee. Where are they? Now unzip the tent. Tell us everything.

JACQUELINE SAPHRA

Keep Ithaka Always in Your Mind:
On the Journey and the Value of Poetry

There is one poem I carry inside me always: one that saved my soul at a difficult time and gave me the tools to move forward in my life and my work. This poem has proved to me over and over again that poetry – wild, priceless and unquantifiable – can be of lasting value to both writer and reader.

When this poem landed in my lap, I was the mother of four young children and had moved on from a successful career as a playwright. I had been toiling as a screenwriter in the sweaty forges of development hell in the film industry for some years, a venture begun in hope that had left me feeling hopeless, as project after project was twisted beyond recognition and then binned or burned. I was ready to give it all up; not just screenwriting, but writing itself, my constant companion since early childhood. People I loved were well aware I was going through this dark night of the soul but they could not help me, I believed. I had to help myself.

I decided to spend a few days away from home trying to gather my thoughts and figure out what to do with my life, during which an unidentified someone sent me a short excerpt of a poem:

> Keep Ithaka always in your mind.
> Arriving there is what you are destined for.
> But do not hurry the journey at all.
> Better if it lasts for years …

Reading this poem was like hearing a fanfare, or like witnessing a million lights go on all at once. Reader, I cried: partly regretting the narrow path I had been walking through life, blinkered, not looking left or right, and partly because I remembered what writing used to feel like; how it was to inhabit the chaos, to revel in the experiments and discoveries, to be open and present, to know those hours when time loses all meaning. I hadn't experienced that fugue state, that sense of creative abandon, in years.

The central message of the little excerpt, which is from Cavafy's celebrated poem 'Ithaka', written in 1911, that trope of the journey being more important than the arrival, of process being more important than product, is almost too often quoted these days; yet it is so hard to absorb that reality when you are living under late-stage capitalism, where art is commodified just like anything else. But the quality of distilled, metaphorical magic in 'Ithaka', the precise but utterly natural mode of expression even in translation, seemed to deliver the message directly into my bloodstream like a shot of adrenaline. Every time I return to this poem (and I return to it often), I feel that jolt of realisation again but differently, depending upon what is happening in both my life and my work. This is where poetry is indeed excellent value, the gift that keeps on giving; you can revisit a great poem again and again and experience something new.

Poetry, with all of its crazy and stubborn heart, vigorously resists all the demands to deliver itself as product to the poet. The poem will never arrive, perfect and whole, or even imperfect and broken, just because you are summoning it. Sometimes it will not arrive at all. The poem takes its time and poem time is different to all other time. Poetry will never buy you mansions: it will almost certainly not make you famous or even popular, but it will offer you *the journey*. And it is always the journey, however bumpy and difficult, that is the reward. In fact the difficulties and challenges are intrinsic and necessary to the feeling of abandon and ecstasy. After all, without these, Cavafy suggests, you would never have set off in the first place.

Poetry didn't come to me immediately after those few days away and all the tears, catharsis and revelation. For quite some time there was much faffing, fear and prevarication because I didn't yet understand that poetry was the place I needed to go to, let alone how to get there. Additionally, as any poet will tell you, the *poetry portal* (as I'm fond of describing it) will often refuse to open however long you've been a writer. But I can report that after all these years I have learned to accept that I'm not the one in charge.

Eventually, following the arrival of the eponymous poem in my life, something shifted and, about ten years later, during a long (and still continuing) process of self-education and obsessive reading, I published my first collection, which brought with it the firm understanding that when I need to express or fully experience something, the place to go is the poem.

But the value of poetry to the writer does not lie in pure self-expression, but in alchemy: "There is always something to be made of pain", wrote Louise Glück. Poetry can turn the base metal of experience into the gold of art, weaving something beautiful and medicinal out of grief or rage, creating something lasting out of joy and love so it can be relived, not just by me the poet, but sometimes, if I'm lucky and hit the right spot, by readers too. So many poems besides Cavafy's have helped me navigate my life. For example, Charles Causley's 'Eden Rock' and Tony Hoagland's final collection *Priest Turned Therapist Treats Fear of God* helped me truly engage with the evanescence of life, Lucille Clifton's 'won't you celebrate with me?' taught me about the persistence of joy in the face of oppression, and Audre Lorde, Denise Levertov and Marge Piercy's poems taught me about political activism and solidarity. As Sharon Olds puts it, "Poets are like steam valves, where the ordinary feelings of ordinary people can escape and be shown."

I've never experienced the connection with readers more keenly than when I set myself the task of writing a sonnet a day during the first lockdown of the Covid pandemic. This was a project I devised to keep myself sane the only way I knew how, to give myself some structure in an unstructured time. It was all about the journey: just coming up with those fourteen lines every day was my only objective. In my reports from my study in lockdown London, I was rapidly taking the pulse of the day, often responding to the latest news or headline or charting my internal weather. Occasionally I shared these drafts and I began to receive messages from people who resonated with them. I started to feel the remote but palpable power of a community of readership. There was also the familiar, tensile strength in the compression created by a musical and precise received form like the sonnet: a means of immediate and direct communication. Form is a tried and tested way of engendering "that / which arrives at the intellect / by way of the heart" as R. S. Thomas put it. While I was working on this this sequence I began to imagine myself as walking a parallel path with the person who delivers meals on wheels, providing a different kind of nourishment, performing a service. I sometimes think that the highest praise a poem can receive is that it affirms or recognises the experience of a reader, although of course it can have many other uses and functions. As the poet Naomi Shihab Nye says:

> As a direct line to human feeling, empathic experience, genuine language and detail, poetry is everything that headline news is not. It takes us inside situations, helps us imagine life from more than one perspective, honours imagery and metaphor – those great tools of thought – and deepens our confidence in a meaningful world.

And, indeed, reading the news doesn't create that meaningful experience: the news lacks the alchemy of poetry; it's one-dimensional, it's factual, it's opinion; your daily paper doesn't have the power of metaphor, compression, mystery, nor the power of direct emotional precision; the news cannot put a

healing or galvanising hand on the place that hurts. As William
Carlos Williams wrote:

> It is difficult
> to get the news from poems
>   yet men die miserably every day
>   for lack
> of what is found there.

Most of us can memorise a poem and allow the magic to keep
working as the poem becomes a part of us. There is no other
art form so complete that it can live inside the self like that.
Often in my classes, older students can recite reams of formal
poetry that they resented being forced to learn as children –
but they are so glad of the comfort of it now! It is well known
that Nelson Mandela, when imprisoned, would regularly
recite the poem 'Invictus' (meaning 'unconquerable'), written
by William Ernest Henley in 1875, to bolster his courage and
determination. A musical, metric poem fat with rhyme, it is an
easy one to hold in your memory in times of adversity:

> In the fell clutch of circumstance
>   I have not winced nor cried aloud.
> Under the bludgeonings of chance
>   My head is bloody, but unbowed.

The Russian dissident poet Anna Akhmatova memorised her
own long poem *Requiem* as she wrote it and burnt the paper
drafts. In this great work, she exposed the terrors of Stalin's
Gulag and the suffering of the Russian people. In the opening
section, Akhmatova writes about an encounter with a woman
whose lips are "blue with cold" as she waits in the prison
queue outside where her own son is incarcerated during the
"frightening years" of the Yezhov terror.

                              Jolted out of the torpor
characteristic of all of us, she said into my ear
(everyone whispered there) – "Could one ever describe
this?" And I answered – "I can."

It would have been a huge risk to keep drafts of this very long
work on paper. So not only did Akhmatova memorise her
poem, but, in case of her capture and execution, she taught
it to her closest friends, insisting they learn new drafts as she
updated it, in painstaking, comma-accurate detail.

The publication of *Requiem* abroad, years before it appeared in
the Soviet Union, brought the reality of Stalin's regime of torture,
repression and murder to the outside world. Demonstrably,
the poet can be an effective messenger feared by totalitarian
regimes and, to this day, it remains a dangerous role: in 2020, for
example, the poet Khet Thi was tortured to death by the military
junta in Myanmar and, as I write, the Sri Lankan poet Ahnaf
Jazeem has been imprisoned without charge for more than a
year. The horrors of the continuing censorship, persecution and
imprisonment of poets is absolute proof of the enduring value
of poetry, affecting hearts and minds, speaking truth to power,
singing into the darkness and silence.

It is often said that poetry is a secular form of prayer,
which explains why people go to it during important rites
of passage – birth, marriage, death – as a way of ritualising
experience, as a source of commonality, a way of creating
and holding community. Friends and family often ask me for
recommendations at these times and, inevitably, I've been
called upon to write my fair share of epithalamiums (poems
in celebration of marriage) and poems in memoriam. My
relatives have discovered that having a poet in the family can
be surprisingly valuable to them. But then I have been equally
surprised to discover that the poetry lovers in my family can be
just as valuable, in their turn, to me.

In fact, after that week I'd taken myself away during my creative crisis and had my close encounter with Cavafy, I returned home in a flurry of thrill and excitement, poised to communicate my epiphany to my family, ready to announce that a poem had changed my life. Who had thought to send this message? Who could possibly have understood what I needed? Reader, the messenger was the very man who opened the door and held out his arms to me: I was married to him.

 Writing Exercise

Describe a place you remember very well and long to return to. It doesn't have to be exotic, or even distant. It may be a literal place or a metaphorical one, but ideally it will come to be both as your poem unfolds.

List the obstacles, internal and external, mythical, factual, practical, emotional, that prevent you from going back to your chosen place.

Imagine making the journey to the place. Describe the route in detail. Include all the locations – real and imagined – that you might pass or visit on the way. Linger and experience those places with all your senses.

Let the poem decide whether or not you reach your destination or whether the arrival actually matters; let the poem decide where to end itself.

KHAIRANI BAROKKA

Poem-making as Anticolonial Assemblage: On the Decolonisation of Poetry

"Decolonization brings about the repatriation of Indigenous land
and life; it is not a metaphor for other things we want to do to
improve our societies and schools." – Eve Tuck and K. Wayne Yang,
'Decolonization is not a metaphor' (2012)

When asked to write about decolonisation and poetry-making
– as decolonisation, internal and external, is a fundamental part
of why I write – I knew I had to begin with the above quote by
Tuck and Yang, writing back against North American settler
colonialism. The word 'decolonise' has become a buzzword,
and is sadly often removed from the revolutionary struggles
that birthed it, struggles that continue, against the occupation
of stolen land from Australia to Canada to West Papua to the
States, against anti-Blackness and false normativities.

'Decolonisation' is often removed from acknowledgement
of past and continued trauma, resilience and communities
of care before 'care', too, became a buzzword in colonial arts
institutions. To de-colonise, to my mind, must continue to
mean de-theft, de-murder, de-assault, de-unlawfully occupy.
We must go beyond decolonising and be *anticolonial*. For that
is what is at stake here, and what continues to bear the brunt
of colonial practices: our very bodyminds, and those of our
communities. And poetry, poem-making, is inextricable from
living in this world, in which obscene wealth is unlawfully
gained and reparations are owed.

For what colonisation has done and continues to do is
the systematic wreckage of communities, and communal
forms of beauty. Whole languages. Whole poetries. Whole
ceremonies including those poetries. Whole mediums and

jokes and intricacies and ancestral betrayals and soothings. Over centuries – whether forced kidnapping of Indigenous children from their communities, including forced schooling and forced forgetting of languages around the world. Whether a globalising of Shakespeare while local bards and traditions remain unstudied. Whether a funnelling of resources away from the so-called 'developing world', the world I come from, that is plundered violently to serve Western lifestyles, Western schools, and artmaking institutions. In the words of artist Barby Asante, "If we really decolonised these institutions, they wouldn't exist."

At its best, for me, poetry – for poetry is always a plural, always a vast plurality and pluriverse of poetries – feels like a tearing apart of *those* processes of destruction. At its best, poetry is to me a wanting-to-dismantle, a disabusing of illusion. And a reassemblage. A galvanisation, a call. When I read Fitri Nganthi Wani or Wendy Trevino, for instance, it feels like cellular liberation. An exhale. An affirmation of truths, a *you aren't alone, the world has been burning for so very long, and how strange it is to try to live here.*

Writing poems in the moment is a fury-storm of love and vexation, and when you're in it, really in it, it is a ride that focusses you wholly. And after, when you look at the page, it is a chance to tell someone they are not alone, whether or not you know it. I have written things I'd thought no one could understand – "but then", as James Baldwin wrote, "you read".

And as to learn is always to begin, I trust poetry enough now to know it can help me try to reclaim. To learn more Minang and Javanese verse to understand my spiritual and cultural heritages. To keep reading banned poets. To keep reading from my home town of Jakarta, and from D/deaf and disabled languages. To have the chance to pass this poetry on to peers and learn from them, thus weaving again something that was supposed to have been destroyed. A poem in indigenous languages is an artifact of non-destruction. Surviving in a body designated for harm is an artefact of non-destruction. A poem by a body-mind targeted for theft of joy can be the glorious presence of possibility not yet usurped.

Poetry for me is a ghost story: a tale of how poetry returns to spectre-visit – and in doing so banishes, for just enough time, many other, less welcome, spirits made flesh. A favourite haunting, recurring.

It began as air.

The first thing I remember writing creatively: a rhyming couplet, as a toddler. Easy enough for children to think of rhymes; surrounded by them in song and books as we are. All children, I believe, are natural poets. If lucky, not socialised to turn from this impulse. If lucky enough to have had an encouraging environment – such as the parents who taught me to read at two, with handmade signs around the house, denoting that 'tangga', for instance, were stairs – perhaps thinking of something like "The sound of the wind / is very, very thin", as I did then.

I clung to writing, exalted in performing – and then incurred debilitating anxiety and self-doubt about the ability to do both. A worrying about one's ability to do something prevents one from delving deep, into the all-forgiving joy of the thing itself. The practice. And it happens to so many of us, how the adult ghouls of comparison and self-hate infect, then prevent, the doing of. Not very many years after I began writing in earnest – whether with the zine my neighbours Franda Li, Peng Wu and I created in elementary school, or on my own – I, along with millions of my Indonesian peers before, during and since, lost a part of our childhood.

What colonisation, what imperialism does, is to create the following feelings across billions of people: *I am in danger, I am hurt, I am alone.* I have felt this often in my life, as I think many have: peril, pain, solitude.

And for a little girl of around eight years old, living under Soeharto's New Order dictatorship in Indonesia – installed by Western forces via a genocide of suspected leftists – imperialism hurt where it mattered most to a child: my imagination. We were subjected by the state to hyperviolent media and imagery and myths. Though my activist parents did all they could, living as a child under censorship – and, essentially, under state emotional abuse in schools – expression, double meanings and being able to say how I really felt formed a ball of enormous, fear-filled struggle. And so, though I wrote into adulthood, it was a difficult path. recognising I came second place in a national poetry competition as a child to a boy's prize-winning sexist poem; hiding from difficult circumstances in the translated and Indonesian words of poets; wrestling with how my imagination, and my belief in it as safe, had been hurt deeply.

The *act* of poem-making, however, persisted, and continued to help vanquish any tenacious demons. Finally, in adulthood, I learned to embrace it fully.

Poetry led me to protection, in a very material sense. However, I will always acknowledge that a certain kind of poetry lent me more material protection in this colonial capitalist world: poetry in written and spoken English, written overwhelmingly 'as an individual', and mostly for audiences that, as international as they may be, include people in the West. Not the writing and performing of communal pantun poetry that animates Minang community gatherings and weddings – often with no commercial purpose. All this is an outgrowth of colonial education systems, and capital flows towards some cultural forms as products and not others. Part of the process that has rushed and continues to rush so many languages towards extinction.

Not all poetries are valued equally under capitalism, or even recognised. Thus, my relationship to English poetry is both love-filled and complicated, as is my relationship to Indonesian poetry, Indonesian language, too, colonising other languages in the archipelago. But the words are there to guide your understandings of the complications along.

Poem-making is not constrained to the act of sounding out or writing or signing words – it's everything that leads up to the spark of the poem pushing through, to that open door where it feels like you're shaping the soul of something. And it's everything during those lulls when you think you're 'doing nothing', when really a poem is brewing its storm and reeling you in, the long game.

Poetry is my promise to a held breath of anxiety that there is air on the other side. Writing poems is the flush of release that can leave me sobbing and utterly thrilled. Writing poetry is the act of telling my soulbody (as I call my bodymind) that it's okay to take that line of thought self-deemed as too hideous or strident or angry to exist. And say simply: it exists.

So take it from there, says the line on the page or spoken or signed, do with me what you will. Make me an epic poem. Make of me haiku. Post me for media companies to own but also for people you care about (our daily bread). Show no one but your great-aunt on her birthday. Or make me disappear. Put me in your sock and walk around with me all day, so I can spark the next line that will become a page you work on for ten years or five minutes, share with a group.

We bear witness to ourselves. Poems guide ourselves to gifts. In my case, the gift of having been born into a military capitalist dictatorship but raised by activist parents is that I was always forced to read with a critical eye, from very young. And to never accept things at face value, to dig deeper.

Trauma fragments minds. But those fragments are beauty in and of themselves. I've been trying to order them to beauty-form my whole life. At its best, poetry is itself resistance to certain neurotypical understandings, Enlightenment-fed, of order and rationality. It is how we make a tower from what we have. A lake. A dagger. Out of supposedly thin air. Out of what to the unimaginative mind is a mess.

Trauma and fragment become, through poetry, montage and assembly. Putting things together again, never as they were. Assembling people, communities, new art forms, in a multisensory way.

If you want skilful compression of complex concepts, interwoven in ways that leave you gobsmacked and breathless, look no further than the best of poetry. And what's 'best' to each person is never uniform, and rarely reflected by what is considered 'best' by ableist, Eurocentric, Western-centric, Anglophone authorities who might proclaim that their 'best' comprises all poetry ever written, anywhere.

I write poetry because storytelling is power, even if you are your only audience. Because conveying emotion, throwing it into a language form of beauty-orb, is a form of healing, of rupture to potentially self-eating machineries: anxiety and unexpressed grief.

Because I believe anger and calm and awe and despair all belong in poetry – most of all, complexity belongs in and is poetry – and that a poem is a prism of endless refractions, that will give you a different set of facets throughout your life, this one 'small' piece of art, and that, miraculously, will

147

give everyone who accesses it different prisms as well. Poem-prisms that change, shift, grow, expand, connect, give rise to experiences and people you would never meet otherwise.

Once released, a poem will never be beholden to just your understandings of what it means. And so poetry is lesson in both loyalty and what it means to fully embrace letting go of control over your creations. This is how we sow connection.

A poem you write, and a poem you read, can give you more of what you have thought lost, what you have been deprived of, what you have been seeking. A poem that incites anger or revulsion or dislike in you can give you the potency to counter-poem.

You can do it. Write a poem. And another. The ability to do so will not leave you, no matter how many times you think it has.

For so long, I felt held down in water, that I could not counter anything. But I could, and I can, and affirming that, amidst so many doubts, is the daily challenge of all poem-makers. And anyone can join us.

I write poetry because it's my 'against'. It's my not 'diminished', my 'remember we have this'.

We are not priests or soothsayers (unless you identify as either!), but we may try towards truths felt in the bodymind. And what comes out is often surprising.

I write poetry because every time the tickle of a verse begins in the body, I have no idea whether this one will take twenty minutes or ten years to reach a form I'm happy with sharing – and if that isn't love and commitment, I don't know what is. Poetry has taught me plenty about love, for others and for self. It's patience, and surprise, all at once.

I write poetry because it surprised me with being such a lynchpin in my ongoing salvation. Because I suppressed poetry for so long, and instead of slapping me in the face for doing so, it opened – opens – endlessly. Love for poem-ing transcends the annoyances, petty grievances and politics present in poetry as in any other creative industry, and I remind myself that these stumbling blocks within poetry as industry are messages: prompts, to counter-poem.

Because poetry is an art form like any other, it is not immune to injustices, discrimination, the privileging of corrosive viewpoints, certain nepotism, and on and on. And if you are engaged in poetry as community long enough, you will be tempted from time to time to mistake all of that noise for the same thing that opens you.

But they are not the same.

Please remember that (a) the poetry business is not the same as (b) offering your insides to a page or a breath on a cellular level, something that breaks you bare and lifts you for the duration of poem-making, poem-reading, that allows you communion with others on an honest level. Keep returning to the vessel of the latter. When dealing with the former, remember to find poetry compatriots who offer mutual respect, warmth and, above all, kindness.

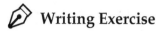 **Writing Exercise**

Remember a time when you read, heard or witnessed a lie related to colonialism, environmental injustice and/or another facet of structural injustice – whether spoken by a politician, written by a journalist, uttered by a passer-by, tweeted by a troll, baked on a cake, printed on a bumper sticker, sung in a song (and so on!). Write a poem about this – notice what changes in your bodymind as you remember it, and feel free to draw on that, should you wish to.

When you've completed a draft, read it, and notice what's happening in your thoughts, feelings and physical body. Journal about this. Remember what was happening in your bodymind during the process of writing the poem. What was being channeled? How do you feel about it? What does it make you want to do? What can you do today?

JENNIFER WONG

Language and Identity:
On Writing Towards the Untranslatable

Growing up in Cantonese-speaking Hong Kong (a former British colony which is now part of China), I often wondered about my identity as a reader and writer. Although I speak Chinese and to a certain extent think Chinese, I love reading poetry and fiction in English, and it is in this world of English books where I found my refuge and freedom. Today, as a writer, I strive to capture my many journeys and discoveries as I move between different languages, cultures and histories.

When writing 回家 Letters Home, I wanted to translate the world in which I once lived: Hong Kong – the only world I knew before arriving in England ten years ago. Hong Kong – a place that's always on my mind even after all this time. But how to share with readers my version of the city? How to bring back the names and significance of the streets, the shops, the food, the secrets in the family, the preoccupations of the locals, their day-to-day triumphs and struggles? And now that I've lived in England for over a decade – having studied literature here, fell in love here, got married and gave birth to my daughter here – what does my adopted homeland mean to me? How do I map my experiences and feelings across two such different places?

I believe that a good poem has the power to translate knowledge into something new, something so authentic and believable that you feel you can touch it, own it.

Poetry is a practice of perception. As such, I'm a keen collector of detail: names, fragments of pop culture, descriptions, notes in museums and exhibitions. Often, I'm inspired by visual impressions and objects. To arrive at my parents' version of 1970s Hong Kong in 'Chung Kiu Department Store: a love story', I trawled through family albums as well as images of Hong Kong streetscapes, immersing myself in the history of the place to translate it for the reader into a world where young people "wear ombre sunglasses / and trumpet-shaped jeans", roast "chicken wings in Tai Tam", and sing Simon & Garfunkel.

Translating taste
Food makes us nostalgic. It brings us back to a moment of intensity, to the attentive preparation of the meal, to the company we cherish or the thoughts that fill our minds when we eat.

To me, food memories are part of the fabric of my personal narrative. A recollection of food is often encapsulated within a larger socio-historical or political context. For example, when writing 'Trace', I began by thinking about one of the most popular dishes in Hong Kong: char siu (barbecued pork). In the poem, I'm amused at how enjoying a meal of char siu rice in a local cha chaan teng (café) is seen as 'common' or working class. What does a Hong Kong person think about when tucking into their char siu rice? And what are the preoccupations of an overseas Chinese person enjoying the same dish thousands of miles from her home country? Like me, perhaps she is thinking about the protests back home, worried about her family and friends.

Can everything be translated?
The experience of speaking Chinese at home, while reading and writing creatively in English, has prompted me to reflect on what language means to me as a poet, the infinite possibilities and freedom in language, as well as the parts of our experience and imagination that cannot be fully translated.

For example, in 'Ba Jin' – a poem that pays tribute to one of the greatest Chinese novelists of the twentieth century and author of the classic novel *Family* – I kept many of the Chinese words as untranslated characters because I wanted to evoke a sense of history that a reader of Chinese literature would feel when considering the poignancy of words like '家'. The word also evokes Ba Jin's life as a Chinese writer who has lived abroad and returned, along with the profound nature of his novels:

> 1923. When you left Sichuan, your *jia*, what were you thinking? 家 is home, or family, or none of those.

To a certain extent, everything personal is untranslatable because of its complexity and subjectivity, and yet there is beauty in rendering this sense of the opaque to a reader, of reaching out for meanings. It is through the act of articulation or approximation that we can unravel or rediscover the rich layers of meaning of an image or symbol.

Research as revelation

From my point of view, researching a poem is often the most enjoyable part of the process. There are so many ways research can deepen the poet's knowledge of what to write about. While working in Hong Kong as a writer-in-residence at Lingnan University, I wrote the first draft of 'Mountain City', a poem central to my poetry collection, which traces the city's landscape and recent history through fragments. It is a long poem that has evolved over several years. Part of my research for the piece involved the rediscovery of local places –from the civil marriage registry on Cotton Tree Drive to the Happy Valley Racecourse. I also looked into the history of districts such as Yaumatei, Tuen Mun and Causeway Bay. Then I turned all this research into an impressionistic collage, selecting images, names and locations that fascinated me because they said something about the everyday moments of local people, from the young boy at the bus stop drinking Vitasoy, to a bride's ornate embroidered dress (lungfung kwa) at a Chinese wedding banquet.

When I wrote 'The King of Kowloon', I went online to research the graffiti made by the legendary Tsang Tsou-choi, who painted Chinese calligraphy throughout Hong Kong. I sieved through hundreds of images, comparing what he wrote across different locations, and so the poem contains some of the mysterious graffiti documenting the life of the artist and activist crowned 'The King of Kowloon'. At the same time, I paid attention to the visual properties and style of Tsang's art, and read reviews of his work, to gain a better understanding of his aesthetics.

Writing the difficult
Certain themes are more difficult to write about than others: political conflicts, betrayals, personal and historical trauma, dystopian visions, injustice, anger and even hatred.

It took me a long time to write about my mother, because of the mixture of feelings I have about our relationship. My need for affirmation and my fear of disappointing her weigh heavy. I remember how painful it was to write 'To a little girl in a village home I never met'. Growing up, there was so much that I didn't know about my mother, or didn't understand back then. So in order to write about her, I drew up a list of what I knew and what I didn't know. I knew, for example, that her mother couldn't read or write, and that her father suffered from mental illness after he fled to Hong Kong during the civil war in the 1940s (*"Just call HSBC if you / need money and they will give you. Plenty."*).

It wasn't until I started writing 回家 *Letters Home* that I began to piece together the jigsaw of my mother's childhood. I kept coming back to her oral accounts of her own family. There were inevitably a lot of gaps in the narrative, which I filled with my imagination. I also realised how different our childhoods were:

How on earth your mother escaped from Shandong
to Kowloon and survived, I couldn't imagine.
The day I stood in a gown at the Sheldonian,
listened to all that Latin, I couldn't shrug off
this girl I never met, who never finished
the village primary and used to stare
at the sea all day, dreaming of Australia.

Writing the poem in the form of a letter allowed me to create distance between myself and the subject matter, and this helped me get closer to a kind of truth.

Sometimes, when narrating complex or difficult matters, I find it helpful to create a more visible scaffolding or structure. Repetition, for example, can be a very powerful way of drawing the reader's attention. In 'Confessions of a minority student', I divide up the poem into two columns, where "success" – in a lighter font – is repeated in the second column as the source of anxiety that preys on the student's mind.

In the prose poem 'My father who taught me how to fold serviette penguins', I use slashes to structure the portrait, drawing attention to the fragmentary nature or spontaneity of thought:

My father, who taught me how to fold serviette penguins

I was eight or nine when I saw you practise / folding serviette penguins. For a long time, / Christmas was a matter of watching fireworks on television / mother trying / not to let her feelings show. / And those evenings you came home / too tired to speak / your voice already spent with the customers. / Thirteen hours of pacing around dining rooms / impeccable cutlery well-ironed table linen other families' / happiness under the chandeliers / that's what work is, has been, for you / since you turned eighteen / and for all the fathers in the golden eighties / it's been a hard day's night / a husband must provide /as long as he is alive. I try to think about / who you really were, a schoolboy before duty / your father who never offered your mother / a kind word, a kiss / but he kept a white shiny statue of Mao / long after the cult was over. / You never finished high school / because your father said / he couldn't tolerate the idea of excessive schooling, a sign of / moral corruption or 嘥錢. / The day I was accepted for the school / on 1 Jordan Road, where the school drive glittered with Mercedes, we knew / we were moving beyond our league. / And yet, and yet, it suddenly seemed / as if something was brightening again in you / something that has nothing to do with table napkins

Editing to translate and transform

After finishing a draft of a poem, I always move away from it. For me, this is a vital part of the overall process of 'making'. I take time out for a long walk, or to watch Netflix, read a book, prepare a meal, or enjoy a leisurely chat with a friend. Only afterwards can I return to my desk with razor-sharp focus, knowing – finally – what I really want to talk about in the poem.

Almost always, the poem I wrote originally turns into something very different after my final edits. For example, 'Trace' – which I talked about earlier – started out as a poem about a Chinese friend who hates Chinatown, even though she often craves Chinese food. Eventually, the real idea behind the poem became clear to me: it was actually meant to explore my friend's mixed feelings about being or feeling Chinese, her cultural and political ambivalence.

More generally, I pay attention to the first and the last word in each line of a poem because that's where the reader gets a chance to pause, where one thought leads to another, and where patterns emerge. The editing process also allows me to rethink where the poem itself should finish. Sometimes, I even move the last line to the beginning or vice versa! In this way, each line or each turn of phrase acts like a stepping stone when crossing a river. Your line of vision changes as you move from one stepping stone to another. When you finish the edit – or reach the far bank – you can look back to the other side of the river and, in one clear sweep, take in the poem's entirety, its beginning and its end.

 Writing Exercise

Choose a year of personal significance (e.g. the year you were born, the first year of secondary school, the year your parents were married).

Jot down any events of emotional significance in your family's history or your own life that happened during that year.

Now do some research. Dig up some information from the internet about what happened that year, narrowing down your search to specific incidents where possible.

Feel free to go in any direction. For example, you may decide to write about the music, bands and records you listened to that year, or you might prefer to focus on a particular family trip.

RACHEL MANN

Waiting to Begin:
On Commitment and Community

In Nikos Kazantzakis's classic novel *The Last Temptation* –
which inspired Martin Scorsese's *The Last Temptation of Christ*
– there is a scene in which Jesus says, "God loves me. I know
God loves me. I wish he'd stop." It is one of those crisp bits of
speech that can lodge in the brain. To my surprise it bubbled
up as I began this essay. Although striking, Kazantzakis's lines
on the face of it seem to have little to do with why I or anyone
might write poetry. I also want to be clear: I've no desire to
compare myself to Christ. Heaven forfend! So what is the
connection my unconscious brain made between those lines
and writing poetry? Well, I have come to see that I've spent a
good deal of my adult life trying to escape from the exacting
demands of writing poetry. I want to translate Kazantzakis's
lines into, "Poetry loves me. I know poetry loves me. I wish it
would stop." As soon as I do that, I think, "Well, that's a little
over the top. Stop being a drama queen!" (I *am* a drama queen!)
However, my translation captures something. It has force. Why
do I write poetry? Well, one reason is because it – whatever *it*
is – bloody well won't let me go. If I could stop, I think I would.

I say this not to be discouraging. Rather, I want to acknowledge
just how primal, for me, the work of a poet is. Perhaps the most
important word in that sentence is 'work'. Poetry writing is
work. It impacts and changes the world, just as other kinds
of labour do. I say this *contra* another picture of poetry with
which I was mesmerised when I was young. Before I began
writing poems seriously, and perhaps even for the first few
years when I tried out the claim 'I am a poet' tentatively on the
tip of my tongue, I was a bit romantic about poetry. I would
talk about art and muses and capital 'I' inspiration. I was

tempted to dignify 'romantic' with a capital 'R'. Well, that was then, and this is now. These days, the beating, fleshy heart of poetry lies for me in 'craft', and in a deeply-embodied work of crafting at that.

I'm not saying that being a poet doesn't involve inspiration – there have been occasions when a poem has seemingly fallen into my pen from the gods – but too often when poets and critics have spoken of the 'art of poetry' I think they just want to elevate some writers and demean others. Power and class are deployed to say, *This is poetry and, more to the point, that stuff over there is not*. No. While there is room for art, part of the wonder of writing poetry lies in how it invites the writer to become a practitioner, as well as to become part of a community of makers and creators. I have come to take seriously the idea that I – a minor poet wrangling with language as best she can – belong to traditions of craftspeople who over time and history have shared skills and techniques, who have trained and supported one another, and are part of a living tradition that not only remembers from where it's come, but also seeks to improvise a fresh future.

As I write the above there's a part of me – a younger, more cocksure, and brittle part of me – that shakes her head; this younger poet asks me, "Did you really just talk about tradition and craft and community and skills?" I don't mind admitting that I'm a little haunted by that younger poetic version of myself. I was a relative latecomer to writing poems. The trigger for my poems was a period of serious ill-health in my late twenties. Quite understandably I wanted to make sense of the collapse of my comfortable way of going on. I wanted to articulate loss. I wanted to learn to be 'me' in new ways. I wanted to write into and speak into my distress, and let's be clear – trauma and crisis are quite legitimate spurs to writing. Indeed, there is a case to be made for the claim that poetry's precision and incision is the only form adequate to speak into such extreme situations. However, I was, in the midst of my distress, impossibly arrogant. I thought the only business of the poet was to 'get it all out'. I thought the poet's job was to express things, either cleverly or wryly or with pathos or comedy and so on. I was sure that just in saying what I had to say, as long as it *looked* like poetry rather than prose, my poems would bowl over anyone who encountered the 'wonders' of my self-expression.

It's pretty hard for me to admit this level of arrogance to you. However, by way of pushback against my cringe and sense of shame about who I was when I started writing poetry, I think I want to say this to anyone starting out on the work of a poet: do not be ashamed of the motors for your writing. The shame or, at a lower level of intensity, the embarrassment one might come to feel later about one's early work serves no great purpose. It adds nothing. My presenting motivation for writing – to articulate my pain and bewilderment – was, no doubt, better than some and worse than others. What matters for anyone who wants to be a poet is that one has taken the absurd risk of starting out.

After that, the challenge is how does one begin to explore the promise wrapped up in such a risky gesture? For me, it lies in diving into the living traditions and conversations and discussions and communities of poetry. In short, read and read and read some more; talk and talk and talk some more; listen and listen and listen some more; write and write and write some more. I say nothing revolutionary here. Indeed, I hope my refrain is one that is echoed in many other contributions to this book: if you want to be a poet engage with as much poetry by others as you ever write. Dare to find your place in old traditions and dare to be freaked-out and annoyed, even pissed-off by poets and poetry. Seek out poets who frighten, annoy or intimidate you, and figure out why. Figure out why you love some things and are left cold by others, and wrestle with stuff that is held up as 'canon' or iconic, not least to see what happens to you as reader and writer. One always receives far more than one can give. Most of all, if you can, do this work of wrestling and formation in the company of others. They are not your competitors. They are colleagues and fellow travellers. Even the most experienced poet is trying to figure out what they might say next. There are many poets who, frankly, are not for me, and who do things and make poems which I would not want to attempt to write. Yet it has been in encounters with their work that I've often been changed the most. In an era where computer algorithms offer music listeners selections which offer narrowing fields – "we think you will also like …" – why not make a conscious effort to break the algorithm? Taste is great. Roving is better. To put it another way: if, as I've suggested, the work of a poet is about being part of an open-ended, living craft with traditions and dead ends and leading edges, why the hell wouldn't one want to take the risk of getting lost and then finding one's way? So often I think poetry is a kind of determined, conscious pressure applied to the possibilities of words and lines and syntax, a work of "just how far can I go before I lose sense" or before I discover a new possibility in language that I never imagined was there. If that's true, one needs guides and friends and fellow explorers. One needs to remember that one can never really expect to go the edge of the possible and *come back* without the support of a host of others. If one does come back, one can never be quite the same.

In reading I have discovered new friends. Some of these are alive and some are dead. I have encountered long-dead voices which speak into my own and answer back and, who to my surprise, permit me to answer back to them. Sometimes, even if the famous dead poets don't seem to want me to answer back, sod them. I will not be serene and obedient. As poets, you and I can speak with Herbert and Donne and they with us. And, of course, more than that, one finds a kind of secular communion of saints, a great cloud of witnesses, living and dead, in the company of the poets. No poet whom one can read is ever truly dead, but I also know that I would be lost without the living community of poets. If the notion of 'finding my voice' has been rather overplayed in poetry circles, the critical conversation of poet friends has been and remains crucial to my development as a mature poet. If reading has helped me locate myself and therefore find myself as a writer, the intervention of friends (in workshops, on courses, through mentoring) has dared me to go deeper and further than I could possibly imagine.

One story which reveals this: as I was starting out to write the poems which became my first full collection, I will never forget a decisive intervention by a poet-cum-friend-cum-mentor who, as I waited for his feedback on another handful of well-crafted, competent poems I'd shared, looked at me nonplussed. I said, "Oh God. What is it? Are they no good?" He said, "No. They're fine. I'm just waiting for you to begin."

Here I come to the nub, I think: "I'm waiting for you to begin." Each of us, as poets, will face particular and personal challenges specific to our own contexts. However, I think my friend's challenge takes us to a fundamental: once we have taken the decision to start writing poetry seriously are we *truly* prepared "to begin", by which I mean is one really prepared to commit to the adventure of the poet's craft? If that sounds dramatic, it's meant to. What I gesture towards is the idea that when we start out on a project or adventure or vocation we can't know what it will cost. We can start something, be very serious about it, but only later realise that we haven't yet fully begun. In my own case, my friend-cum-mentor discerned something which I wasn't entirely prepared to face: my fear of failure. I'd worked and worked to achieve a level of skill and technique in my poetry which led to a certain level of recognition; I'd found a way to produce good poems. However, having achieved a certain level, what I wanted was to stay still.

To retrench. I wanted praise or applause or acknowledgement for my achievement. I wanted the world to say, "Rachel, this is very good. Well done, good and faithful poet." What I was scared of was the next step: the step into the unknown, into danger and – here it is – the step which held the prospect and possibility of failure.

I like to think that I am less scared of failure now. Well, that's what I tell myself. I am certainly more sure about trying to reach for the edge of my skill and of such talent as I have. I realised, through the encouragement of my mentor-cum-friend, that if I was ever going to be the poet I *could* be and *wanted* to be, I had to be prepared to risk it all. I had to let go of my competence and be prepared to write bad poems. More than that, I had to dare to write poems which might be actively disliked or be dead ends. I've spent so much of my writing life wanting to be the poetry equivalent of a celebrity 'lookie-likie'. I've wanted the safety of writing poetry which imitates what is currently seen as good. That's okay as far as it goes, but ultimately such an approach fails to trust in the particular body and specific stories I am. If my poems are bad or good or indifferent or disliked, at least now I can begin to say they are my poems, and, on good days, I can even say that I remain thankful that poetry will not let me go.

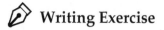 **Writing Exercise**

Our bodies are something with which we are both intimate and from which we are often estranged. They can be sites of glory and hope as well as trauma and pain. Write a poem about a body – your own or someone else's. Spend a few minutes to map out the body with all the words you associate with it – nouns, adjectives, verbs and adverbs. Make this mapping exercise as physical as possible.

Perhaps write from the point of view of a part of your body you either love or fear; or write out a story of your body that is in need of celebration or healing.

Make the poem as grounded and – good body word – as visceral as you dare. If you hit a blockage as you write, perhaps try to make a list poem: "This body is not ...", "This body might ...", "This body is ...", and so on.

HAFSAH ANEELA BASHIR

I Have Only My Pen, My Voice and My Heart: On Writing to Bear Witness

"What's the point of recording my stories? What will you gain from it? What will change? Joh hogaya voh hogaya."
- Sarwari Begum (my 91-year-old grandmother) answering journalist Sarfraz Manzoor for *The Times'* article 'Deadly partition: 70 years after the British exit from India' (13 August 2017)

Ever since I could hold a pen and write my own name in cursive script, I have been acutely observant of everything around me. One of five children in our London household, my childhood was rowdy and eventful. With three of us siblings born in the month of August, three years in a row, my voice wasn't always heard among a headstrong brother and a dominating sister. I would often quieten down, sit back and just watch as a scene unfolded, an active observer on the periphery. Here, I learnt the art of noticing.

Because I slowed everything down and observed, I can tell you the exact number of dots in one row of the plastic lino walkway that covered the brown carpet connecting our dining room to our kitchen, where my parents were often in the midst of a heated argument.

Trying to remember huge chunks of my life has been a challenge. Love. Rebellion. Twenty-five years of marriage. Migration. Motherhood. Career. Friendships. Divorce. Successes. I have spent a lifetime listening to, collecting, documenting, holding and embracing the sacred stories of people around me and finding ethical ways to share them. But invited to write this essay, I realised that so much of my own experience has been lost to time through that age-old notion that we must forget in order to remember.

Poetry, for me, has been an archiving of sorts. A vault that houses the emotional truth of memory. One where the past, present and future can collapse into a solitary poem, enabling me to voice my own experiences and also dive into the stories of others.

Writing to bear witness started consciously for me in my twenties. A young hedonistic mother, I had just discovered the sweetness of faith. In 2001, I moved from England to Lahore with my four young children, hoping to connect to my roots, immerse myself in a culture I felt distanced from, and enjoy all that my parent's motherland had to offer.

Starting my new life coincided with the United States' invasion of Afghanistan. According to Western media, the motive was to oust the Taliban and liberate all the veiled women in the name of freedom and democracy. As my neighbouring country was bombed relentlessly during Ramadan, the sense of injustice loomed large and to process my feelings I turned to writing.

A shift occurred. I started to write about what was happening to others. By doing so, I learnt so much about what was happening to me – how I was changing and growing.

I wrote poetry that spoke to the stark class divide in Pakistan. The poverty. The gender expectations. The bombings. The lives of ethnic minorities. The deaths. I also explored the country's rich and diverse culture – its food, music and effervescent markets. I never forgot (as in the poem 'Jasmine') that I was a British Pakistani writing from the periphery:

> Scent of *motiyah* floats through thick smog, settles
> near flickering red traffic lights.
> > How local beggars and rouged men in silken
> > saris have ensnared them!
> > How, with barbed wire, they have pierced each
> > flower's delicate hymen!

How the soft bracelets adorn their limp wrists,
wrists that flick matted heads!

Little girl not working fast enough, the corner of
Cavalry ground.
How her bangles rap against car windows,
not quite hard enough, not quite grabbing
attention.
How she sings *pachas rupee baji, pachas rupee!*
Peering into me, as she leans towards
the cavern of my car.

I had just given birth to my fifth child in the National Hospital of Lahore in Pakistan. My chest was rattling with infection and the small electric heater placed in my room by a nurse was not helping. The coughing was pulling on my C-section stitches and I wanted to return to the comfort of my house, where my four children were waiting in anticipation for their little brother. It would be another two days before they discharged me. Sitting in a clinical office on the downstairs floor, with my new baby on my lap, a doctor was telling me that my chest X-ray showed I had pneumonia. Ten minutes later my husband declared that, as dire as the news was, he had no choice but to return to work in England on the next available flight.

I remember the room becoming unbearable. The white dusty fan creaked as it revolved slowly. My voice stuck in the bottleneck of my throat and a heat was gathering in my chest. My husband asked why I wasn't saying anything. The walls were a crisp white, paint peeled in the corners, some of it scattered on the floor like crushed confetti. I slowly opened my purse and pulled out a receipt for some shoes I'd bought long ago.

I started to write.

My husband pressed me to not ignore him. I carried on writing, tiny words in blue biro describing the stifling situation and how the spark in my chest was raging and that if I opened my mouth I would not be able to control the wildfire. He left the room to clear the hospital bill. My lips made no attempt to move, accustomed as they were to unfruitful conversations, but ink continued to fill the little paper rectangle. For years, I kept the note in my purse as a reminder of what Maya Angelou once said: *When someone shows you who they are, believe them.* I still have those scraps of testimony, alongside many others.

Some moments of testimony have honoured a friendship. Three years ago, I watched my best friend's mother draw her last breath in the early hours of a serene morning. Sadiah held her mother's hand with such tenderness as she encouraged her to declare the shahada and bear witness to God's oneness. I watched a solitary tear fall from her mother's eyes and we all whispered prayers around her until her soul left that room. It was the first time I had witnessed a death and the experience led to a poem called 'Rani', my friend's mother's name, which means 'queen'. During my book launch in 2018, Sadiah's cries of gratitude and grief accompanied me as I read the poem:

> *Your husband props up your pillow / hoists you a little upright*
> *to stop you disappearing under the white shroud.*
> *He chews the delicate flesh of an apple between his teeth / and*
> *places it in your mouth as if you're Eve.*

To bear witness is to name. And I have done this for as long as I can remember because I consider it to be part of my own spiritual journey. Whether it be to humanise the four boys killed in 2014 by Israeli naval fire while playing football on a Gazan beach, or to give a name and identity to the housemaid whose body was found on an empty plot in Defence Lahore. Whether it's to make sure the accounts of my 91-year-old grandmother's partition experiences are documented for future generations, or simply to capture the funny statements my children said as toddlers. Whether I'm documenting the struggles and celebrations of marginalised women, or remembering the young black men and women killed at the hands of the police in the US and the UK, bearing witness, for me, has meant honouring the life and the name of another human being so that their story is hopefully not lost to history. Also, in contrast to journalists, who usually try to erase themselves in order to report as objectively as possible, I prefer to present a more intimate voice on the page – one that comes from an active and reflective life.

No doubt this passion is fostered from belonging to a faith where we are birthed not only bearing witness to God's oneness but also to the responsibility that comes with the act of witnessing. For me, this has always been intrinsically linked to testifying for the sake of truth and justice – what we call in Urdu and Arabic *Haqq*. In the Qur'an we are instructed 'stand firm against injustice even if it be against yourselves.'

Whether you "stand firm" through the use of your hands, with your voice or deep within your heart, I believe it is important to speak truth to power. Over the years, I have learnt to have courage and use my voice, my words and my poetry to communicate my truth to as many people as possible. As I write this essay, the Israeli military is bombarding the Gaza Strip relentlessly, as they have for decades. Over the past twenty years, as a result of the Israeli–Palestinian conflict, over 3,000 Palestinian children have lost their lives. The most recent operation snatched the lives of two Israeli and sixty-three Palestinian children. As a mother of five myself, these numbers keep me awake at night. For a believer, our affection, mercy and compassion for each other means we feel as one body: "When any limb aches, the whole body reacts with sleeplessness and fever." It is through this fever that I try to make sense of it all. In writing to bear witness, I have only my pen, my voice and my heart – from this the poetry comes.

THE WAR-TORN CHILD

I will tell God everything
The sharp metal pieces
Taken out of my stomach
Will all come with me

I will tell God everything
The men with the guns
And the aeroplanes of fire
Will all get into trouble

I will tell God everything
And ask if the lightening in the sky
Was Him taking photos
If not, I'll give him my drawings

I will tell God everything
That Mama's face was gone
But I found Baba's feet
And put them together like shoes

 Writing Exercise

Whenever I am finding it difficult to write a poem, I go to a
quiet place to ground myself. I think about three things I have
seen or experienced that I have not yet found the words for. I
then choose one of these, take my pen and write.

What does it mean to acknowledge and bring into existence
that one time when both my warring adult sons were diligently
planting with their bare hands, together, the tree my neighbour

had thrown out for the rubbish tip? They both chose to save it and designate a place for it in my garden. In silence, as one poured water at the root of the tree, the other dug. Where one hollowed the ground, the other positioned the tree. Both took turns to lean against the wall when tired and I couldn't help but feel both hope and love as I bore witness to this. This is a poem I still need to write.

When you give it a go, think about the small details, what happened and how you felt as the event unfolded. What do you yet need to bear witness to?

CLARE SHAW

Poetry Saved My Life:
On Writing About Trauma

"There is no greater agony than bearing an untold story inside you," wrote Maya Angelou. *I Know Why the Caged Bird Sings* tells the story of her early childhood and is the first in a series of seven autobiographical books which chart her life through gendered violence, sexual abuse and rape, racial trauma, and poverty. Maya Angelou knows why the caged bird sings, but I'm not sure I do. Is it a call for help, a cry of despair, a biological instinct? Or is there never more need for us to pour out our hearts – to be heard, to be beautiful – than when we are caged or in pain?

> A light song of light is not sung
> in the light; what would be the point?
>
> (Kei Miller, 'Light Song of Light')

Why do we sing our songs in the darkness? Why do we write our trauma? Perhaps because research documents the benefits of expressive and creative writing. Blood pressure, lung and liver function, school grades, memory, mood and sporting performance – all show significant improvements as a result of regular writing practice. Writing, according to research, can also help you live with the effects of trauma[10]. Perhaps writing can even save your life.

Let me explain. I was flying to Oslo and the plane began to cough, quietly at first, then increasing until there was a stutter then a hush. Even the crew were screaming as the sea rose towards us very fast. It was terrible, terrible; I had to write a letter of goodbye to my daughter but my pen was shaking so

---

10. Karen A. Baikie and Kay Wilhelm, 'Emotional and physical health benefits of expressive writing', *Advances in Psychiatric Treatment*.

much it began to glow (maybe I was pushing down too hard?) red-hot and bright. Perhaps it was love, perhaps grief, sheer will to survive – all that I know is that by its light the engines were restarted, the flight path reset, and we took to the skies, higher and more glorious than ever before.

Or perhaps we could refer to a theoretical model of trauma. Although 'trauma' is based in the Greek word for wound, these days it is more likely to describe the emotional impact of a terrible event. The word came into common usage as a result of Freud, who framed trauma as an emotional experience which is too much to bear or make sense of – the sort of event, like a violent assault, bereavement or natural disaster, which can destroy all that we understood about ourselves, the world, and our place within it. Suddenly, it seems, the ground is not beneath my feet, the sky is not where I left it. Suddenly I learn that no one can save me, I was never safe.

> *On 4th July, 1990, at 10:30 in the morning, I went for a walk along a peaceful looking country road in a village outside Grenoble, France. It was a gorgeous day, and I didn't envy my husband, Tom, who had to stay inside and work on a manuscript with the French colleague of his. I sang to myself as I set out, stopping to pet a goat and picking few wild strawberries along the way. About an hour and a half later, I was lying face down in a muddy creek bed at the bottom of a dark ravine, struggling to stay alive.*
> – Susan Brison, *Aftermath: Violence and the Remaking of a Self*

How, when the river has spilled over its banks, when planes fall from the sky, when a man has a knife to your throat, when a terrible virus means you can't step outside of your own house, can writing save you?

Catharsis – or, as it's most commonly known, 'getting it all out' – was first coined by Aristotle. He believed that watching tragedy on the stage allowed the audience to be purged of their feelings of fear and sadness – just as Plato argued that poetry was a kind of wordy Epsom salts which can 'cleanse' the body of painful feelings. Similarly, in Freudian terms, catharsis involves telling your traumatic story and allowing yourself to experience the emotions connected with it until you are free from those feelings.

But recalling trauma really hurts. Far from saving you, it has the potential to sink you. In 2017, Erin Vincent published the article 'They say writing is cathartic, but writing about my parents dying almost killed me' (*The Guardian*). I've long felt wary of the assumption that simply talking about or reliving our traumas can overcome them. There's a whole lot more to it than that.

My concern comes from a very personal place. I grew up with a story of myself as the black sheep of the family – clever, sensitive, or just weird. As a teenager, this story explained my eating disorder and my self-injury. As my emotional state deteriorated and my coping strategies grew more desperate, it was decided that I was not just sensitive but mentally ill. I lived with that 'truth' until I came to a new story – I was surviving, in the best way I could, the emotional consequences of childhood rape, and a chaotic, neglectful and at times abusive family.

Other members of my family continue to tell a very different story. Perhaps this is why Muriel Rukeyser says that "The universe is made of stories, / not of atoms." Perhaps this is why writing after trauma can reimpose a sense of order when order is shattered. Perhaps it offers us a richer, more meaningful, less harmful alternative to the language of diagnosis. Or perhaps I am really mad, or too clever for my own good, too loud, too much. Perhaps it really is true that I was born into darkness and I use my words to drag people down with me.

However dark they are, we need our stories. A story binds a million separate moments together. As my mum descended into dementia, her inability to make sense of stories meant that she could no longer make sense of the world. Her favourite telly programmes became just a series of disconnected scenes – just like her life and her sense of self. Stories give us coherence and identity. We are raised with a certain story of ourselves: we may live happily with that story all our lives, or we reach a point where it no longer 'fits'. That point might come about as the result of trauma, the sort of event which, in Susan Brison's words, "shatters one's fundamental assumptions about the world and one's safety in it" and "severs the sustaining connection between the self and the rest of humanity".

It's a process of liberation and loss. When what we took for granted has been transformed, we can find ourselves in a world in which nothing makes sense or feels safe. And at this point we can come to the possibility that we can tell our own stories and create our own truths. Here, perhaps, lies the saving, sustaining, transforming potential of words – especially, in my opinion, poetry. Consider, for example, the work of Tadeusz Różewicz, a Polish guerilla fighter who wrote about his experiences during the war. 'In the Middle of Life' (1956) is a kind of anti-poem: a poem stripped of its usual devices of metre and metaphor, but which is magical and painful in its capacity to capture the effect of – and the slow recovery from – trauma:

> this is a table I kept saying
> this is a table
> on the table are bread knife
> the knife is used for cutting bread
> people feed on bread

Gregory Orr (2002) writes of this poem: "Różewicz,'s 'I' rebuilds both world and self *with* and *through* language." This is a table, he repeats, urgently building his understanding of the world as benign … knives are for cutting bread he tells himself, and not for hurting people. Orr concludes: "[D]eep in the recesses of the human spirit, there is some instinct to rebuild the web of meanings with the same quiet determination we witness in the garden spider as it repairs the threads wind and weather have torn."

This is a table, this is a knife. This is a tree and this is a path. The path is lined with ferns and shadows; they are equally beautiful. Perhaps I laid my words down and they were a path I could follow. Perhaps they led me into the forest, perhaps they led me all around it. Perhaps I walked from that dark place alone, I left that story behind, perhaps I rewrote me. Here's one of mine:

Total Social Isolation in Monkeys

After a while, says Monkey, I learned to accept it.
I stopped trying to climb the walls.
Time became malleable
and largely irrelevant.
There's no pressure to sleep at night.
When I find my own pace,
the day is a lake I can float in quite gently.
And the day is incredibly long
and surprisingly busy.
I am a house with many rooms
and the rooms are all filled
with fruit. It's okay to be insane –
some of the visions are pleasant,
my thoughts are extraordinary.
I touch myself very adeptly
and the walls are safety.
It's not as silent as you might expect.
I recite poetry in various forms,
I speak with demons. I am learning
to embrace my own company.
Though lacking resources, I have time.
There's a great deal in here left to learn.

This poem is taken from my 2022 collection *Towards a General Theory of Love*. The collection includes a series of poems about Monkey – a character who emerged from my interest in Harry Harlow's experiments on baby rhesus monkeys. Carried out through the fifties and sixties, these profoundly controversial experiments played a crucial role in establishing the importance of attachment and maternal care by subjecting monkeys to extreme psychological suffering. The persona of Monkey offered me a vehicle through which I could interrogate my own experiences of trauma, neglect, loss and, more recently, the social isolation of lockdown.

Adopting the voice of Monkey in *Towards a General Theory*, or a bus shelter and an orangutan in *Straight Ahead*; using the metaphor of natural disaster to describe personal catastrophe in *Flood*; or interweaving my own story with film narrative in *Head On* are all devices which allowed me to keep an emotional distance from trauma, whilst engaging with it more deeply, directly and honestly than I could otherwise have managed. As I recently wrote in the free resource 'My Story, My Words: A Practical Guide to Creative Writing for Survivors of Sexual Abuse and Violence', "[W]e don't always have to describe experiences directly. In fact, sometimes our writing is more powerful when we approach it indirectly – as the poet Emily Dickinson said, 'Tell the Truth but tell it Slant'." Using metaphor doesn't make our writing less truthful, or less powerful. Consider this extract from Kim Moore's astonishing poem 'When I Open':

> will my wild things come back, will the horse
> of my legs and the dragon of my ribs,
> and the gentle sheep which lived in my throat
>
> like a breath of mist and the silverfish
> of my eyes and the skylarks of my hands
> and the wolf of my heart, will they all come back
> and live here again, now that he's left[.]

Metaphor and imagery are just two of the devices the poet works with: we also draw on white space and line break, form and structure; punctuation, font and grammar; rhyme, rhythm and allusion; and juxtaposition and contradiction. Our tools are nuanced and various, and as Katrina Naomi's article 'Responding to Violence' (*Magma*, 62) makes clear, they are also very powerful. Naomi offers the reader three poems about an experience of attempted rape, written over several years, and though they all describe the same attack, they are very different in tone, style and content. One is written in the imagined persona of a young man; another describes her experience directly, in plain language, with little punctuation and no breaks; another makes use of imagery and describes her attacker as a crocodile. Writing in different ways at different times allows Katrina to explore different aspects of her story, and to tell that story in the way that feels right for her.

Within this process, structure and form can play an important enabling role: sometimes, birds sing *because* of the cage. Note that 'Social Isolation in Monkeys' has regular five-line stanzas, which cohere through the use of internal rhyme and a conversational but deliberate rhythm: sometimes the poem is a sort of cage, sometimes a cage is a way of being held. Sometimes the constraints of form and structure allow us to engage with trauma in poetry by setting limits to what can otherwise feel like overwhelming stories and immense emotions – by building a structure or scaffold to hold experiences we cannot hold for ourselves:

> In the dark times
> Will there also be singing?
> Yes, there will be singing
> About the dark times.
> (Bertolt Brecht, 'Motto')

Since I received an invitation to write this chapter, the world has changed – so much so that, in writing this sentence, I was lost for words. Trauma is not an individual experience, nor is it the preserve of combat veterans, those who have lived through famine and disaster, survivors of violence and abuse. "The world has changed" is not adequate, but perhaps the story is still being written. Since March 2020, we have all survived trauma on a universal scale: the sudden shattering of our shared realities and sense of safety. We have lost 3.9 million people, and rising: every time I drafted this paragraph, the number had risen. Another hundred thousand. Another three hundred thousand. We lost jobs and homes, assumed roles and expected futures, workplaces and friendships, cultures and ways of life.

But we did not lose poetry. In fact, we discovered that we needed poetry more than ever before – its ability to console and connect, to express sorrow, to find beauty, to create meaning where sense and structure has been stripped away. We wrote and read, and when we were too tired and anxious to read, we listened. We rose to the challenge of moving our groups and workshops, our readings and festivals online. We sang in the darkness, we sang in our separate houses; in the dark times, we sang of the darkness, and we will continue to sing of that darkness until we find the words to hold it and bear it, and we will continue to sing of the light.

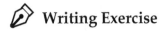 **Writing Exercise**

Instructions for Surviving a Pandemic

In this exercise, you'll be invited to write about living through the pandemic. If this works for you, you can use the same exercise to write about other traumas you may have experienced.

Step 1
Using the freewriting technique, write down three things you did that helped you to get through the experience of Covid. It might be something very healthy, like exercising and meditation. Or, like me, you might have eaten the contents of your fridge whilst watching Netflix. Either way, you survived, and this exercise is about honouring your survival.

> I drank plenty of beer
> I watched Netflix into the small hours
> I went for a walk every day

If you're writing in a group, you might want to share your examples.

Step 2
Now write down those three examples as instructions:

> Drink plenty of beer
> Watch Netflix into the small hours
> Walk every day

Step 3
Now keep on writing. If you find it easier to work with prompts, try writing for just sixty seconds on the things you did in each of these settings:

at home
in work
in the morning
in your neighbourhood
with friends and family
last thing at night

Step 4
You should end up with a list of 'Instructions for Surviving a Pandemic'. You can repeat this exercise, using the same steps and prompts, to write about the strategies you've used to help you live with other traumatic experiences. Remember to go with your first thoughts – the more unexpected and contradictory your strategies, the better.

RISHI DASTIDAR

Become a Different Bird:
On Changing Your Poetry
(And Maybe Also You)

Back in the days when I used to think it was a good thing to be an early adopter of social media platforms (especially the little bird one), I always would struggle as to what to put in the profile section of those apps and sites. (On reflection, it was probably an early proving ground for any skills of concision I may or may not have – 'describe yourself in 140 characters or less!'). The thing I ultimately settled on was using the word 'Restless', like so.

Partly because I think I thought it made me sound deeper and more profound than I am. Partly because it meant I didn't really have to think about crafting something bespoke each time, because I'm lazy. Partly because it meant I didn't have to think (which perhaps also gives you an insight into how deep and profound I am). But also partly because it's true.

Ah, but: *what kind of restless?* How did, how might have this single word actually manifested in my life? What was I restless about? What was I restless for?

If I was a skilled enough liar, at this point I would say: adventure! The world! I have traversed continents, conquered cities, bent oceans to my whim, made my bed in forests and sand dunes, lost my heart to skies; braided my ambition and vanity together to forge a career that has taken me around the globe, made me love and be loved many times over, with only minimal pain and maximum gain.

Ahem. Mostly, what I have been restless for is: the new. New people and places, to a point. But more than that: the sensation of newness, the thrilling fizzing, the prickle of hair standing up on skin as you bump into some thing you haven't before: a texture of a sound, a colour on a wall, an arrangement of words, an economic theorem, a political idea.

I am a neophiliac. This is not necessarily a good thing.

I mostly used to get this from pop music. Then I discovered poetry. And thank goodness I did, as I think it's marginally more dignified to be feeding my addiction from poems than whatever might be number 7 on Spotify's Viral 50 Global playlist. Marginally.

*

It probably helps that my way into contemporary poetry, Durs Grünbein, is what I would call a 'kinetic' writer (and yes, I am aware that *all* writing is at some level kinetic, in that it functions to get us from the beginning of what it is saying to the end of what it is saying; and if it is really good, it will encourage us to then go back and do it again, maybe even read it in a different direction).

What I'm specifically thinking about here is: arranging words on a page in certain way that gives the feeling of motion. You might call it being animated, dynamic, lively even. "Can the thousand little wires in its fur / Sate the ravenous ape who's so quick to learn?", Grünbein asks in 'Biological Waltz', and what I see there is a) those wires vibrating, thrumming with possibilities and b) that being the only way this particular ape (not that he's especially quick to learn [and I yes I am using this image in full knowledge of what it suggests, about me]) might be sated. If neophiliacs ever are.

Of course, there are technical ways that we can discuss another time to release and realise this energy down the page when you are writing your poems (hint: your line breaks, verb choices and any neologisms are very good for this). But what I want to impress upon you more right now is: motion is good.

Kinetic energy is the force that changes the world (physicists, I know this is wrong, but give me this one, eh?) And kinetic energy is at the core of nearly all the poetry I like. Yes, of course I can appreciate the perfectly-crafted vignette, a still scene, an exploration of a moment of tenderness, heartbreak, or despair. What I like more, however, is when I can detect that some thing – some motion – is going to happen, even in the midst of stasis:

> It's true: there is light at the centre of my body.
> If I could, I would lift aside a curtain of this flesh
> And demonstrate, but for now it is my private neon.
>
> (John McCullough, 'Soulcraft')

Or, from another poem that I keep in my wallet:

> We have short time to stay, as you,
> We have as short a spring;
> As quick a growth to meet decay,
> As you, or anything.
>
> (Robert Herrick, 'To Daffodils')

*

Some of you, smarter than me, will have by now detected that I am using 'motion' as a euphemism for 'change'.

We could go further, and suggest that 'motion' is also a euphemism for 'new' and so I want you to keep the "make it new" dictum close to you whenever you are writing anything. But I think you know this already.

*

I know there are some poets who know from early on what they are going to write about, and how, and then they continue to mine those seams profitably for the rest of as long as they like. God I envy them.

The rest of us are in much more of a whirl, as we try and find our *it*s, from in our lives, in our loves, in our jobs, in what we stumble across, what we observe deliberately, what we might cultivate from the fragments of language we hoard.

Hello hedgehog, meet fox. (For those of you that don't know: "a fox knows many things, but a hedgehog knows one big thing," as Archilochus put it.)

I'm not gonna say 'be more fox', even though by temperament, instinct and training I am a fox, because I suspect being a hedgehog is pretty cool as well. But: I want you to say yes to knowing lots of things; useless things, trivial things, arcane things, highly-specialised things, abstract things, things that mark you out as first name on the pub quiz team-sheet.

Curiosity is an attitude you can live by. It's certainly one that the best writers write by.

*

Never forget: poetry is a way of thinking as much as it is a mode of expression. Done well, the exploration of it can answer lots of the questions you have about life – yours, and everyone else's – not just the initial enquiries that impelled you – compelled you – to write.

And with curiosity hopefully also comes a sense of playfulness. The practice of contemporary poetry doesn't often lend itself to play (and I'm not saying you should suddenly aspire to become a gag merchant or a stand-up comedian).

Playfulness – and not being too precious about your work or your process, at least while you are creating – is both valuable and vital in creating work that has energy, that moves. Take your ideas for walks, runs, ambles, shuffles – whatever works to get them moving.

*

Let's come back to "make it new". What's more interesting is if we can add to the *it* at this point. *The it that is you.*

I feel an epigrammatic dictum coming on, that you might wish to keep above your desk and use: *As much as what you write about changes, the you that writes the poems should also be changing.*

Of course, we are all always changing, and we can't really do much about that. What we can start to do is tune into those changes, and let it affect how we write, what we write about, consciously.

Yes, I mean ageing and embracing all aspects of what that means for how, what and why we write. Especially the bit of ageing that means we trust our instincts a bit more, and our rational brains bit less.

An example: I had various different versions of *Saffron Jack* knocking about for over 10 years. When I could bear to drag the manuscript out of the bottom drawer (and my goodness I had to steel myself to do that), the metamorphosis that it was going through was obvious: from dramatic monologue to piece of prose to blank verse; none working, but all experimented with as I a) tried to solve the problem of what the final form would be; and b) tried to solve this problem within – no, beyond – the skills and capabilities I had at the time.

And when I did finally come to solve it, about eight years on from having first had the glimmers of the idea, it was through: a) having the experience to trust the instinct that the thing that I'd read that had so excited me because it was new to me (in form and content) would be the answer that I was looking for; and b) having the confidence to go for it.

Two things I wouldn't have done earlier in my writing life. Even though the final version looks and sounds odd. *Especially* because the final version looks and sounds odd.

My *odd* of course might be your *new*. That could be an intriguing spirit with which to approach your reading and writing.

*

I should also confess at this point: I have a terribly low boredom threshold. Which is in part why I am a neophiliac. To that end: why would I try to write the same poem, about the same subject(s) again? God bless you if you can, and you can find your chosen subject(s) endlessly fascinating, and then communicate that to the world. I get exhausted just thinking about that prospect.

I should be less fox, maybe.

*

This does also mean that I'm very alert to repeating myself a) in terms of subject and b) voice. I can't be the only poet that's looked at a 17th draft of something and gone: "Oh fuck, why do I sound like me?" In some cases that means there isn't an 18th draft. In others that means the 18th draft is better. The odd thing is that you can never tell which way it is going to go.

Another epigram: *The poet's real challenge is to sound like themselves while never saying the same thing twice.*

My attempt at solving this conundrum right now is to try and be a bit less rich and fluid in how I write, inhabit characters more – invent them – and generally try and get as far away from the me that could be any 'I' that makes it into a draft.

Oh, did no one tell you that? You are allowed to pretend here, to get into a character, to write about characters. Writers of fiction aren't the only ones allowed that fun. Don a new suit, become a new person. (Once, at university, I spent a term wearing a three-piece suit, and carrying a furled umbrella all the time. It wasn't really me. But it was a bit of me, that I still miss.)

*

Ultimately, what we are talking about here is: finding a process that means you can keep writing about what you want to write about for as long as you want to write about it, in a manner that keeps the exercise creatively interesting for you, and hopefully rewarding for your readers. If you are managing to create art as part of that, which in some way advances conversations, changes minds, launches new ideas into the world, provides clarity, compassion and hope to people, then even better.

(You should always be ambitious for your words.)

"I used to think I wrote because there was something I wanted to say. Then I thought, 'I will continue to write because I have not yet said what I wanted to say'; but I know now I continue to write because I have not yet heard what I have been listening to." – Mary Ruefle

*

Three final notes to leave you with. First: to misquote Edna St Vincent Millay: "I will put Change into fourteen lines". Or more as you wish.

Second: You have to invent yourself as a poet. So it makes sense that you might have to *reinvent* yourself as well; and more often than you might recognise.

Third: here's Mary Ruefle again: "I believe all poets are winged, and some can fly and some cannot, and that having wings is their distinguishing feature, not whether they can fly. Some poets can fly but they don't have wings and they are worse. If you are trying to fly, stop it. Just watch under your arms for signs of wings, and if they sprout, even if you can't make it off the ground, say you are a turkey – well, that is an interesting thing. Of course you may be a lark, and that would be lucky."

Become a different bird. Change your wings.

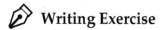 **Writing Exercise**

Take an existing draft; edit it radically so that you could tweet it if you were minded too – that is so it is 280 characters or less.

Take that text, then redraft by expanding it out – hopefully you'll arrive somewhere different, better.

Or maybe the ghosts of the original draft take over again. Try not to let them, too soon.

JONATHAN EDWARDS

The World's Strongest Men:
On Writing About Family

When I think of writing about the family, I think of two key questions that I've been asked at significant times in my writing. The first of these happened twenty years or so ago, in the room of one of my university tutors, who I'd taken a poem to for advice during office hours. I can remember the poem clearly – it was a response to one of my favourite festive television programmes, *The World's Strongest Man*, and imagined one of the huge, lycra-clad and muscle-bound participants strolling into Top Man in a city high street and trying to buy some new duds for a night out. The tutor liked the form of the poem and the approach to language, but then he asked a question that's stuck with me. This isn't an important enough subject, he said. You need to think about what subjects really matter to you. Travel? Romantic love? And what about family? I've been writing some elegies recently about my father. How's your dad? Is he doing okay?

Then, as now, my father was hale, and hearty, an incredible life force. What the tutor said about subjects stuck with me, though, but it was really another ten years or so before I did anything about it. Even then, I don't really feel like I did anything myself, but rather that the subject of family jumped into my poems quite by itself. As the poems of my first collection took shape, I was still, as far as I was concerned, writing about Evel Knievel and football matches, human pyramids, and fantastical folk I spotted on the streets of Newport. Increasingly, though, family was insisting on being a part of these poems, however far away from them the starting point of the writing was. Here's a poem that I wrote at around this time:

Gregory Peck and Sophia Loren in Crumlin for the Filming of *Arabesque*, June 1965

Sunday. The crowd beneath the viaduct
waves banners made from grocery boxes, bedsheets:
Welcome to the valleys Mr Peck!
Wind turns their chapel dresses into floral
parachutes; their perms don't budge an inch.
The emotion of it's too much for one girl's
mascara. *We love you Miss Loren!* My father

parks away from them, around the corner,
in his brand new car, a '30s Lanchester,
with stop-start brakes, a battery he shares
with a neighbour. All sideburns and ideas, a roll-up
behind one ear and a flea in the other
from my gran for missing Eucharist,
he coughs and steps down from the running board,

as two Rolls-Royces pull up opposite.
Gregory Peck, three years after being
Atticus Finch, steps from one, says *Good morning.*
From the other – it isn't! – it *is*, wearing her cheekbones.
My father's breakfast is nervous in his stomach,
but he grabs his *Argus*, pen, and *Yes*, they'll sign.
Her high heels echo away through the whole valley.

That's how my father tells it. Let's gloss over
how his filming dates aren't quite the same as Google's,
the way Sophia Loren formed her Ss
suspiciously like his. Let's look instead
at this photo of the crowd gathered that day,
he walked towards to share those autographs,
his fame. There, front and middle, with her sister,

the girl he hasn't met yet – there. My mother.

At the point of inception, this wasn't a poem about family. I'd come across online a story about the visit of Gregory Peck and Sophia Loren to Crumlin, a village which is about fifteen minutes from where I live. Like all good stories which can inspire writing, there were plenty of holes in it, plenty of places for the imagination to work. A holy book for me, then as now, is David Wojahn's *Mystery Train*, from which I took a great deal of my approach and my desire to write about pop culture. The first stanza of the poem, then, simply creates the scene. I was really quite surprised when my father stepped into the poem – right there, at the end of the first stanza – and began to drive the poem forward. Even more surprising was that my mother jumped in and made the ending for me. For me, endings are everything, the difference between a poem and a non-poem, and I'm the sort of writer that ends up with a hundred unfinished poems, sitting there waiting for endings. When they come, if they work, they can come with a feeling of complete surprise, and this was certainly the case with this poem.

Among things that have been really key for me, in terms of writing about family, then, is actually to write about something else. As with Simon Armitage's poem 'The Last Panda', from his collection *Seeing Stars*, which presents Ringo Starr as a panda, poems can happen when two unlikely things are put together. There are lots of advantages to such an approach, particularly when writing about a well-worn groove like family, which many poets have explored from a wide range of angles. One of these advantages is simply to get you into a room and writing. Writing has to be, above all, a form of entertainment for the writer, something they enjoy doing. Put me in a room and tell me I can write about the 1990s Welsh football team, or Tom Jones, or a 1980s movie, and I'm happy, excited. From there, the serious subject of the poem might emerge. But ask me to write about a serious subject in the first place, and nine times out of ten I'm leaving the room entirely and going out to buy cake.

There's another significant advantage to writing about family by writing about something else, and that's this. In order to write well about family, I think, family has to become representational; it's necessary not just to write about your own family, but about your reader's. What appears very obvious to me is that my father in my poems is not my father. I'm writing about a representative father and a representative relationship which I hope readers can connect with, but there isn't a straightforward relationship between the figures in the poems and my real parents, beyond the fact that the poems express the truth of how I feel about them. Creating some mythological element in poems about family, allowing the characters to become bigger than their real-life selves, was crucial in my first collection. For me, much of that mythology came from pop culture and from the invention of surreal scenarios. Among important influences here was Tom French's 'Touching the Bones', the title poem from his extraordinary first collection, which sets familial grief alongside a television nature programme. Andrew Waterhouse's 'Climbing my Grandfather' and Catherine Smith's 'The Biting Point' are wonderful models of a surreal approach to family. And then there are the endlessly driving inspirations of the most important fathers in our literature, the fathers of Seamus Heaney and Dylan Thomas. Heaney's father is mythologised through everything the rural and farming world gives those poems; Thomas's father is rendered immortal by the poet's extraordinary formal approach.

Another way of saying this is that nothing in my poem about Gregory Peck actually happened: my dad never went to Crumlin that day, and he met my mother for the first time on the bus stop after a dance at the local institute, when he asked her for a chip, or offered her a chip (which way round this really was is a bone of consistent familial tension). I'd tried to write that story about them meeting many times, but it was only when Gregory Peck walked in through the door that it became possible. The only part of this poem which is true in a factual sense is the part about the Lanchester and the fact that my father borrowed a battery from a friend (a guy who worked in the local hotel) every time he wanted to take it out. I'd tried to write a poem straightforwardly about that car, but the detail ended up here, and this is another key thing about writing family poems: the stories that family tell to each other, around the dinner table and in the living room, can generate great ideas for poems.

The thing about family poems, though, is that people will read them as entirely true, even when they're very far from being so. When my first collection came out, some of my dad's friends came round to the house and asked to see the copy of the *South Wales Argus* which had Sophia Loren's signature on it. The poem plays with the veracity of the story within itself, of course, and one form I found quite useful at this time was setting up a story, and then questioning the truth of the story within the poem itself.

All of this brings us to the second significant question I've been asked in relation to family poems. When my first collection appeared, the question I kept getting asked – again and again – at readings and in interviews, was "How do your family feel about the poems?" At first I was baffled by this. Why should they feel anything? They aren't in the poems: I'm writing about *the* family, not about *my* family. Then, as the question kept coming, I started to get annoyed, because it seems to reduce the art. People respond to novels by admiring the writer's craft; people respond to poems by thinking that a writer has simply written down truth, rather than shaping material. Eventually, though, writers I admired started asking this question, and it felt like I should think about it.

Whether or not this had an impact I'm not sure, but one thing that happened in my second collection, as well as retaining the approach to family through pop culture, was to develop an opposite approach. Rather than adding extra layers to family stories to make them into poems, I began to do the opposite, simplifying and reducing the tales told round the dinner table in order to make the poem happen. Such was the case here:

My Father Buying Sweets, 1956

So here he is, eleven, a little bugger,
with his neat curls, his comprehensive training
to be my lookalike. His mother's voice
chases him down the terrace, as he swaggers to the music
of the coins in his pocket: his school tie, flipped
over his shoulder, is a silk scarf sported by an artist,
strutting from one absinthe-joint to another
in 19th-century Paris. Now he looks in the window
of Mrs Bullen's sweet shop:
the reflection puts his face in a jar
of chocolate toffees, grinning. Chimes
announce him as he steps inside, the shop
Mrs Bullen's front room. Fearsome
in pastels, she emerges, eyes him, places weights
on one side of the scales, sweets
on the other, offers him
all she has of justice. A clatter
into the till and he's out
and walking home, a paper bag
full in his palm. There are years
in which the shop will go to bedsits, the bedsits
to ruin, my father's mouth will bloom
with fillings, but now his evening stretches
deliciously ahead, and he pauses helpfully
beneath a streetlight, so we can watch him
lift one gleaming thing from the bag, unwrap it,
raise it to his lips –
so I can taste all the butter, cream, the sugar,
here, on the tip of my tongue.

The family story which generated this poem is much more complicated than what happens in the poem itself. One day, the owner of the sweet shop on the corner made the cunning business decision to increase her profits by beginning to charge a ha'penny for the bag the sweets were put into. On buying the sweets and paying the new price, my father returned home and told my gran what had happened. My gran was the most wonderful woman in the world, with a comic genius the absolute equal of Oscar Wilde's, and she was nobody's fool and nobody's victim on any matter. When she heard the story of the sweet shop, she walked out of the house and the fifty or so yards down the street to the shop. Standing there in front of the counter, she poured the bag of sweets into her apron, slammed the paper bag down on the counter, and demanded the ha'penny back, which the shopkeeper wordlessly reached for in the till and handed back to her. Then my gran walked out, my father trailing behind her, with a wide-open mouth that not even a sweet could close. Even as I write this, I'm sitting here, applauding her.

I tried to write that story many times as a poem, but it never quite worked. The story itself was so strong that there was nothing for me to do as a writer, nothing for me to imagine, no way to involve some famous person or some elaborate, surreal scenario. Unless material is made over in the imagination of the writer, becomes something else, it's very difficult for a poem to breathe its own independent life. What I found, then, was that what the poem wanted was for the family story to be simplified.

In doing so, I found it possible to do a couple of things which sought to elevate and mythologise the now simpler story. One of these was the outlandish metaphor of the absinthe-fuelled artist, which was drawn from biographies of Rimbaud and Wilde. A second – and this is a repeated strategy in my family poems – was the messing about with time frame, the whoosh of movement through time which I love doing and which happens in that sentence beginning 'There are years ...' The poem jumps forward, before returning to the moment. A third happens at that point when 'he pauses helpfully / beneath a streetlight, so we can watch him ...', which was an attempt to break the fourth wall of the poem, drawing attention to the way the writing is framing this moment as a film director might, and explicitly involving the reader.

The second point here, around time frame, is a key one in terms of writing about family, and unifies the two poems I have written about in this essay. Of course, like every writer, I write poems in the hope that one day I might write good poems. Since pretty much all the time I'm not doing that, though, there has to be another reason for trying to write poems. More often than not, when writing about family, I'm using pen and paper for the time travel it provides, and for the opportunity to spend time with my family before I was born. Perhaps this is a result of watching the *Back to the Future* movies at an impressionable age, but if I could step out of this room I'm in now and go anywhere, I'd spend a day hanging out with my father or grandfather (hey, both!) when they were young, because I know we'd have a bloody great time. So much of writing for me is the closest I can get to doing that.

I mention my grandfather here, because the poems I'm currently working on, towards a third collection, dwell on his life. Sometimes, as in the poems I've discussed, they seek to mythologise him, make him larger than life. Sometimes they simplify family stories about him. Sometimes they mess about with time. Whatever else happens in the future, I know I'm going to go on writing about my family. These poems are love letters to the family poems I love by writers like Greta Stoddart, Don Paterson and Sinéad Morrissey. But they are also, endlessly, love letters to members of my family themselves. For all that I'm lying in all of these poems, I'm also trying to write truth, to rise to the challenge of writing something worthy of these people, because no one else will if I don't, and then these people will be lost. Of course, I'll never get to something worthy, but that holy mission keeps you going. Family is the most important subject in the world. I'm writing, after all, about the world's strongest men.

Writing Exercise

Write a poem about your family. Consider selecting from or combining some of the following strategies in the piece that you write.

Try creating a mythology for your poem by combining the subject of family with something else. This could involve drawing on pop culture, on surreal situations, or on exaggerated metaphor to give your characters grandeur.

It's possible to make the marriage of the two very different subjects clear in your title. I've tried things like 'My Family in a Human Pyramid', 'My Family as an Olympic Bobsleigh Team', 'My Father and I as Saturday Lunchtime Tag-team Wrestlers', 'My Family as Characters from *Apocalypse Now*' etc. So try formulating a title which makes the smash-up of subjects clear, and the writing of the poem should simply be an exploration of what that unholy combination might result in.

Do some research into local stories from your area involving famous people, and see if you can insert members of your family into these outlandish narratives.

Think about trying to undermine or question the veracity of the narrative you tell, within the poem itself.

Have a think about family stories which are told around the dinner table, and how these could be used in a poem. It may be possible to elaborate on these stories and make them even more magnificent, but it might also be possible to simplify them, and this might be where the poem is.

Think about time shifts in your poem, and the way that whooshing forwards or back, within a single sentence, can give energy and interest to a poem.

Think about breaking the fourth wall in the poem, talking about the act of writing within the poem, or directly addressing the reader or involving them in the situation.

Write a poem which is simply about imagining or spending time with people you love, before you were born, and dwelling on the moments of empathetic connection between you and the person you're writing about, which can be generated by sharing this experience.

Think carefully about your endings. Hopefully one will come unbidden, as a surprise. Then you know you have a poem!

Enjoy your writing! And spend the time allowing yourself to imagine something pleasurable and exciting so that, whatever happens, the writing itself will have been fun!

PASCALE PETIT

Curing Songs:
On Poetry, Art and Healing

I cannot imagine a life without making poems, but I spent the first part of my life as a sculptor. I suspect I'm continuing to make objects, paintings and installations with words. Image-making is key to my writing practice, as is the need to transform an unhappy childhood, and to express awe of the natural world. I believe that poetry can help, both by revealing beauty, and by transmuting painful experience. I suffered from depression since childhood, and took medication for it when young, but it seems to me that art can be a better support, even sometimes a cure. Might it be possible to make books where suffering is changed by the spell of poems? I stopped making sculptures in my forties but still need to make my poems as physical.

I know the exact point when I confused images with words: it was when I was struggling to learn English at the age of seven. I'd been sent from Paris, where I was born, to live with my grandmother in Mid Wales. Then a great-uncle gave me a pictorial dictionary where every word was accompanied by a picture of what it meant. And that was it, from then on I would always see words as images. My earliest memory of making art was when I was five, when I realised that while I was drawing I was happy. I had trouble writing at that age, because I'd moved countries so often. I wrote letters to my mother in franglais, but every page had a back with drawings. I now think of those drawings as my first poems, my first safe places, and later I would start to create them with words. Writing would become a place where I could change reality and make it my own.

When I was thirteen I was returned to my mother to South Wales, and that was an unhappy time. But I could retreat into creativity to escape from her, as I had done at the Paris infant school. I'd spend as much time in my bedroom as I could, drawing, or writing essays. At school I discovered Keats and the Romantic poets. One of the English teachers recited 'Ode to a Nightingale' in class – the lines seemed to speak directly to me, and showed how luxurious and sensory words could be, as well as holding pain safely. Art could remake the world, be a forest that would grow in my head, and always be there inside.

What I didn't realise until much later was that my mother was severely mentally ill. By the time I was eighteen and started art school, I too was suffering from depression, and was prescribed Valium. By the time I was twenty-two, I was on stronger anti-depressants with serious side effects. In the ten years before my MA course at the Royal College of Art, I alternated between being a sculptor and being a writer. I escaped into the worlds I could create. This world was rich and full-bodied. My guide there was John Keats. I just had to recite 'Ode to a Nightingale' and I was there, among the stanzas of his "airy citadel". His axiom "that almost any man may like the spider spin from his own inwards his own airy citadel" was a lifeline. I loved to be in my studio creating my own world. I'd already taken part in feminist exhibitions in the ten years between my BA and MA courses, and had worked with resin and fibreglass figurative casting, and with glass structures, in a group touring exhibition called Pandora's Box (1984–85). When I left the RCA, I had debts and no studio, so I worked full-time at Clifton Plant Nurseries in Maida Vale. This was formative because even though the hours were long and I had no time to make art, I learnt all about tropical plants. It was a foundation for the forests of my books.

Eventually, I gave up sculpture to concentrate on writing. This meant that the poems had to take the place of sculptures. They still have to be as solid and inhabitable as installations or objects. It wasn't until my early forties that I wrote poems that seemed to help, not just by their subjects but through improving my craft. My first collection, *Heart of a Deer*, went unnoticed and, in retrospect, I think there is too much foliage, too much metaphor. In it I started making ice worlds and forest worlds, in which my parents featured, but I was not explicit about why they were there. There were frozen waterfalls, ice caves, and the Amazon rainforest first appeared after two trips I'd made into Venezuela's Lost World of tepuis (sandstone plateaux) to see Angel Falls – the highest waterfall in the world.

In *Heart of a Deer*, I was taking my sculpture imagery and transposing it into poems. A large glass installation I'd made for Pandora's Box had consisted of a left-hand side of frozen sea glass boxes, and a right-hand side of thorny rainforests and nests. All the foliage in my glass installation was made of painted hawthorn twigs – blue for ice and sea, and green for forest. I thought of my glass 'palace' (echoing Keats's mansions of the mind) as a depiction of the natural world in precarious balance. Or, a mind in precarious balance, trying to keep sane.

Then, just before *Heart of a Deer* was published, my father made contact. He had vanished for thirty-five years. I discovered he lived in Paris in the Latin Quarter and was ill with emphysema, so over a period of two years I visited him. The result of this painful time was my second collection, *The Zoo Father*. It's in this second book that I made some leaps in my craft. The two lessons I learnt from my first book were 1) to be more direct and less vague about my childhood traumas, 2) to write more dynamically. I learnt to do the latter by going to the Ménagerie in the Jardin des Plantes every morning before visiting my father. It was there that I wrote the proto-poem* 'The Zoo Father' that led to the entire book. It was only in this poem that I realised *how* I could write about my abusive father, and the shock of his reappearance only to die. I portrayed him and myself as the Amazonian animals that I observed in the zoo

* Proto-poem: a word conceived by Pascale Petit which refers to a book's original poem; the first poem written that inspires both a new collection and its structure.

and befriended. An animal is dynamic, so my lines leapt about as they did. The proto-poem was later discarded, but in each stanza I'd portrayed us with animal masks, and that became the structure of the book.

It was as if all the trance of making sculptures was transferred onto the page, the special feeling of working in my studio and being so immersed in my world that I wouldn't even hear the phone. It took a long time for me to learn how to do that with words. I still think words are a tricky medium, but I've found strategies to work with them. And I needed to write well, to fill my home with Amazonian books and to spend days in libraries hunting for images and texts that could feed the poems. I was suffering from depression again by then, and on Prozac. I lived alone. My routine was to write all morning, do other work in the afternoons, and I read until last thing each night, so that I'd wake with new images percolating. I kept large notebooks full of cuttings and quotes and first drafts.

It was at this time, in 1999, that I collected clippings and texts about *Victoria amazonica*, the giant water lilies of the Amazon rainforest. I went to Kew Gardens to watch them in the Water Lily House. I copied lines into my notebook, about being "chest deep in muddy water all night, probing the secrets of the lily pools". These lilies are pollinated by beetles, and when I was a sculptor, I'd made life-size casts of a fibreglass woman with beetles around her glass womb and butterflies in her glass brain. Beetles were one of my many obsessions, and I had persuaded zoologists in London's Natural History Museum to give me boxes of iridescent metallic pinned beetles. But I couldn't write that water lily poem.

Fifteen years later I happened to bring those notebooks to Paris with me, to start writing my seventh collection. The pages fell open at the *Victoria amazonica* notes. And that was how I started writing the title poem of *Mama Amazonica*, with my mother as the flower, pollinated by my beetle father. I would wake up very early and work, then go to the Ménagerie or to Vincennes Zoo, which had reopened and where Aramis the black jaguar had been rehoused from his small enclosure at the Fauverie in the Jardin des Plantes. At this time, he was introduced to a young female jaguar, Simara, and she was the model for my mother, 'Jaguar Girl', the second poem in the book.

Those pages in the 1998 notebook eventually enabled me to write a tender collection of poems about my estranged, abused and mentally ill mother. To have this book was redemptive. One of the reasons I write poetry is to transform my life, and that's one of the things this book does: I open it and love a mother who didn't love me and who I couldn't love. It took fifteen years after her death for me to be able to achieve this.

In my eighth collection, *Tiger Girl*, I was ready to write love poems to my grandmother, the person who saved me by bringing me up and in whose garden I flourished. To explore my grandmother's Indian heritage, I went to Indian tiger forests, and saw just how brimming with wildlife they are. While in *Mama Amazonica* my mother's madness is merged with the abuse and precarious health of the Amazon rainforest, in *Tiger Girl* family traumas echo forest traumas: poaching echoes child abuse. I discovered forest wonders. My grandmother told me a tiger once entered the tent where she had been left alone as an infant. I'd seen a jaguar in the Peruvian Amazon, but I'd never seen a wild tiger, so I went to Ranthambore National Park in Rajasthan, and two tiger reserves in Madhya Pradesh – Kanha and Bandhavargh National Parks.

Apart from the wildlife of Central India, I also encountered two of the tribes: the Baiga, who believe they are descended from tigers, and the artistic Gond. Gond art, with its motifs of swamp deer and trees, was a major inspiration. One talisman behind *Tiger Girl* is a book by three Gond artists, *The Night Life of Trees* (Tara Books, 2006). These screen-prints of mythic trees, with their glowing colours on thick black hand-bound paper, accompanied by short texts about their mysterious origin myths, inspired me to write my long poem 'In the Forest', in which I embark on a journey into the tiger forests at night, and sparked other poems, such as 'Trees of Song' and 'The Anthropocene'.

Another artwork behind *Tiger Girl* is Henri Rousseau's painting 'Surprised! (Tiger in a Tropical Storm)'. In my poem 'Surprised!', what I set out to do was to capture the rainstorm across the canvas, to convey the elemental force. I wanted to get as close to a tiger as my grandmother had. And on my second trip, spent entirely in Bandhavgarh, I did! I was within one metre of Spot-T, the queen of Tala Zone. I saw dozens of tigers, but that encounter was magical – we made eye contact!

The more I researched, the more I realised I might be one of the last to see them, and the same goes for leopards, sloth bears and wild elephants. Even owls and Indian rollers have to be protected from poachers and loggers. I also learnt that the forest birds are endangered and used for pujas, as good luck charms. It was shocking to read how much cruelty there is in trapping birds as well as the mammals and reptiles. But I could not conjure the wonder of Indian wildlife without describing how precarious it is.

My poems are acts of remembrance. When I compose, I bring the creature to mind – the flameback woodpecker that flew right past me, what that felt like, the air of its wings against my face, the speed with which it vanished into the air. That's how fast wildlife is disappearing, just a flash and then it's gone. These sense impressions are hard things to grasp, but that is the challenge, and it's worth trying. Poetry was once used to cast spells. Just as our ancestors drew beasts on caves to make them appear, so words were spoken, or sung, to recreate wonder, and heal sickness by evoking the magical. Poetry is a curing song, it was once used for that purpose, and still is in some cultures. I hope readers find my poems pleasurable, not just painful, that they can open *Tiger Girl* and hear the forest speaking.

 Writing Exercise

The Writing Cure

A. Go to a place that fascinates you. It could be a street, a room, a park, a wood, a particular animal, tree or bird, or a painting, installation or a sculpture in a gallery. Spend as much time there as you can. Take a small notebook that fits in your pocket. Take photos. Do research about it if you need to. Make notes about your chosen place or object through all eight senses.

B. Here's a list of senses you could use:
1. Visual: sight, brightness, clarity, colour, motion, pattern, form, depth of field, perspective, and scale.
2. Auditory: hearing, sounds, sonic effects, alliteration, assonance, half rhymes.
3. Olfactory: smell, a powerful evoker of memories, even when others fade.
4. Gustatory: taste, food, eating.
5. Tactile: touch, temperature, texture.
6. Organic: awareness of inner body sensations – heartbeat, pulse, breathing, digestion.
7. Kinaesthesia: awareness of muscle tension, motion, also gravity, mass and density.
8. Synaesthesia: a sense impression produced by another sense – that loud green, her prickly laugh, the blue vowel 'a'.

C. Bring someone important to you into this place. It can be yourself. Perhaps they/you are the object, or an animal, house or tree you've focused on. Do a fast free-write or hot-pen – don't let the pen lift off the page. Keep the censor away! This is your world, your chance to write about something central to you, something you must write about but maybe keep resisting. Let others write about other subjects. You may want to paint the same mountain over and over again, as Paul Cézanne did with Mont Sainte-Victoire. Don't let the inner critics stop you painting better and deeper, in different lights. You are collecting material towards a poem or poems, perhaps even a book.

D. If you don't get anywhere the first time, try again, start afresh, rather than fine-edit. Perhaps there's a line from the previous attempt that feels the most alive, that you could use now as your first line? When you run out of steam, go for a walk, a coffee, whatever helps, and keep at it. Don't throw out any drafts! Collect more info, make more notes. Try using a sense you haven't used yet to move the poem along.

It's important to remember that disappointing drafts are not failures, but the imagination incubating a new creation. Even if this exercise doesn't lead to a poem, it may shift something; it might be feeding your subconscious self. Believe that the poem is there, waiting to be discovered. Follow your obsessions and explore any side paths they lead you to. Remember that research counts, is valuable time spent towards writing, as is reading other poets who inspire you. Put all of yourself into your work. What is it that you have to say, that no one else can? Make time each day, at least one hour. Have fun, however serious the subject: it's playtime. I believe that prolonged, regular time set aside to play can lead to cure.

Further Reading

'How to' guides

52: Write a Poem a Week. Start Now. Keep Going – Jo Bell and guest poets (Nine Arches Press, 2015).

How to be a Poet: A 21st Century Guide to Writing Well – Jo Bell and Jane Commane (Nine Arches Press, 2017).

The Craft: A Guide to Making Poetry Happen in the 21st Century – ed. Rishi Dastidar (Nine Arches Press, 2019).

Cambridge Introduction to Creative Writing – David Morley (Cambridge Introductions to Literature, 2011).

An Introduction to English Poetry – James Fenton (Penguin, 2003).

The Practice of Poetry: Writing Exercises From Poets Who Teach – edited by Robin Behn and Chase Twichell (William Morrow Paperbacks, 1992).

Writing Poems – Peter Sansom (Bloodaxe, 1993).

Writing Poetry – W. N. Herbert (Routledge, 2009).

Essay collections

Stress Fractures: Essays on Poetry – ed. Tom Chivers (Penned in the Margins, 2010).

The Redress of Poetry – Seamus Heaney (Faber & Faber, 2002).

Forgive The Language: Essays on Poets and Poetry – Katy Evans-Bush (Penned in the Margins, 2015).

Madness, Rack, and Honey: Collected Lectures – Mary Ruefle (Wave Books, 2012).

Don't Ask Me What I Mean: Poets in Their Own Words – edited by Don Paterson and Clare Brown (Picador, 2012).

In Their Own Words: Contemporary Poets on their Poetry – edited by Helen Ivory and George Szirtes (Salt Publishing, 2012).

On Poetry – Glyn Maxwell (Oberon Books, 2012 / 2017).

Poetry in the Making: A Handbook for Writing and Teaching – Ted Hughes (Faber & Faber 1967 / 2008).

Strong Words: Modern Poets on Modern Poetry – edited by W. N. Herbert and Matthew Hollis (Bloodaxe, 2000).

On Poetry – Jonathan Davidson (Smith | Doorstop, 2018).

More inspiration

#Afterhours – Inua Ellams (Nine Arches Press, 2017).

Stairs & Whispers: D/deaf and Disbaled Poets Write Back – eds. Sandra Alland, Khairani Barokka, Daniel Sluman (Nine Arches Press, 2017).

101 Sonnets – Don Paterson (Faber & Faber, 2012).

Too Young, Too Loud, Too Different: Poems from Malika's Poetry Kitchen – eds. Maisie Lawrence and Rishi Dastidar (Corsair, 2021).

The Golden Shovel Anthology: New Poems Honoring Gwendolyn Brooks – eds. Dr Peter Kahn, Ravi Shankar, Patricia Smith (University of Arkansas Press, 2017).

The Penguin Book of the Prose Poem: From Baudelaire to Anne Carson – ed. Jeremy Noel-Tod (Penguin, 2019).

Adventures in Form: A Compendium of New Poetic Forms – ed. Tom Chivers (Penned in the Margins, 2012).

Black Nature: Four Centuries of African American Nature Poetry – edited by Camille T. Dungy (University of Georgia Press, 2009)

Ten: Poets of the New Generation – edited by Karen McCarthy Woolf (Bloodaxe, 2017).

Threads – Sandeep Parmar, Nisha Ramayya and Bhanu Kapil (Clinic, 2018).

Poetry journals

Ambit, Butcher's Dog, harana poetry, Magma, PN Review, Poetry Birmingham Literary Journal, Poetry London, The Poetry Review, The North, The Rialto, Under the Radar, Wasafiri.

Contributors

Romalyn Ante is a Filipino-British, Wolverhampton-based author. She is co-founding editor of *harana poetry*, a magazine for poets who write in English as a second or parallel language, and founder of *Tsaá with Roma,* an online interview series with poets and other creatives. Her debut collection, *Antiemetic for Homesickness* (Chatto & Windus), is longlisted for the Dylan Thomas Prize 2021 and shortlisted for the Jhalak Prize 2021. She was recently awarded the Jerwood Compton Poetry Fellowship 2021-2022.

Khairani Barokka is a writer and artist from Jakarta, based in London. Her work has been presented widely internationally, she was *Modern Poetry in Translation's* Inaugural Poet-in-Residence, and she is currently UK Associate Artist at Delfina Foundation and Research Fellow at University of the Arts London. Okka's books include *Stairs and Whispers: D/deaf and Disabled Poets Write Back* (as co-editor), and debut collection *Rope,* both from Nine Arches Press. Her newest book is the collection *Ultimatum Orangutan* (Nine Arches Press).

Hafsah Aneela Bashir is a poet, playwright & performer originally from East London. Co-director of Outside The Frame Arts, she is passionate about championing voices outside the mainstream. Winner of the Jerwood Compton Poetry Fellowship 2019, she is an Associate Artist with The Poetry Exchange, Associate Artist with Oldham Coliseum Theatre, Supported Artist at The Royal Exchange Theatre and a board trustee of Manchester City Of Literature. Her debut poetry collection *The Celox And The Clot* is published by Burning Eye Books. She is the Creative Director of the Poetry Health Service.

Leo Boix is a bilingual Latinx poet born in Argentina who lives in the UK. He is a fellow of The Complete Works Program and codirector of Invisible Presence, an Arts Council England scheme to nurture new voices of Latinx writers in the UK. Boix is the recipient of the Bart Wolffe Poetry Prize 2018 and the Keats-Shelley Prize 2019. His debut English collection *Ballad of a Happy*

Immigrant (Chatto & Windus, 2021) was awarded the Poetry Book Society Wild Card Choice and has appeared on *The Guardian's* 'best recent poetry' list in August 2021.

Vahni Capildeo's eight books and seven pamphlets include *Like a Tree, Walking* (Carcanet, 2021) and *Measures of Expatriation* (Carcanet, 2016), awarded the Forward Prize for Best Collection. Capildeo's interests extend from poetry and non-fiction into intersemiotic translation, traditional masquerade, and collaboration. Recent work includes 'Lighthouse and Anchorage', a journal twinning Edinburgh and Norwich for the UNESCO 'Imagining the City' project based at the National Centre for Writing. Capildeo is Writer in Residence at the University of York and Visiting Scholar at Pembroke College, Cambridge.

Mary Jean Chan is the author of *Flèche*, published by Faber & Faber (2019). *Flèche* won the 2019 Costa Book Award for Poetry and was shortlisted for the International Dylan Thomas Prize and the Seamus Heaney Centre First Collection Poetry Prize. Chan's writings have appeared in *The Guardian Review*, *The Poetry Review* and elsewhere, with criticism published in *The Journal of American Studies* and *The Journal of British and Irish Innovative Poetry*. In Spring 2020, Chan served as guest co-editor alongside Will Harris at *The Poetry Review*. Born and raised in Hong Kong, Chan is currently Senior Lecturer in Creative Writing (Poetry) at Oxford Brookes University.

Jo Clement is the recipient of a Northern Writers' Award and the Managing Editor of *Butcher's Dog* poetry magazine. She holds a PhD in Creative Writing from Newcastle University, awarded an inaugural AHRC Northern Bridge scholarship. Jo has written for *The Travellers' Times* and BBC Radio 4. With support from the European Roma Institute for Arts and Culture, she edited *Wagtail: The Roma Women's Poetry Anthology* (Butcher's Dog Publishing, 2021). Jo currently works as a Creative Writing Lecturer at Northumbria University. Her first book-length collection, *Outlandish,* will be published by Bloodaxe Books in 2022. www.joclement.co.uk

Jane Commane is director/editor at Nine Arches Press, co-editor of *Under the Radar* magazine and co-author (with Jo Bell) of *How to Be a Poet*. Her debut poetry collection, *Assembly Lines* (Bloodaxe, 2018) was longlisted for the 2019 Michael Murphy Memorial Prize. Her poetry has featured in *Staying Human* (Bloodaxe) as well as in *The Guardian, Butcher's Dog* and *Poetry Birmingham Literary Journal*. She is a Writing West Midlands' Room 204 writer, and in 2017 was awarded a Jerwood Compton Poetry Fellowship.

Sarah Corbett has published five collections of poetry, *The Red Wardrobe* (Seren, 1998), shortlisted for the Forward Best First Collection Prize and the T.S. Eliot Prize, *The Witch Bag,* (Seren, 2002), *Other Beasts* (Seren, 2008), the verse-novel, *And She Was* (Pavilion Poetry, 2015), and *A Perfect Mirror* (Pavilion, 2018). She also writes novels, and won a Northern Writer's Award for Fiction in 2019. Sarah is senior lecturer in Creative Writing at Lancaster University, and lives in Hebden Bridge.

A poem from **Rishi Dastidar's** debut *Ticker-tape* was included in *The Forward Book of Poetry 2018*. A pamphlet, *the break of a wave*, was published by Offord Road Books (2019). His second collection, *Saffron Jack*, is published in the UK by Nine Arches Press. He is also editor of *The Craft: A Guide to Making Poetry Happen in the 21st Century* (Nine Arches Press), and co-editor of *Too Young, Too Loud, Too Different: Poems from Malika's Poetry Kitchen* (Corsair).

Jonathan Edwards's first collection, *My Family and Other Superheroes* (Seren, 2014), received the Costa Poetry Award and the Wales Book of the Year People's Choice Award. It was shortlisted for the Fenton Aldeburgh First Collection Prize. His second collection, *Gen* (Seren, 2018), also received the Wales Book of the Year People's Choice Award, and in 2019 his poem about Newport Bridge was shortlisted for the Forward Prize for Best Single Poem. He lives in Crosskeys, South Wales.

Writer and singer with post-punk band The March Violets, **Rosie Garland**'s award-winning work has been published internationally. She has a passion for language nurtured by public libraries, and a firm belief in the power of persistence. Her most recent poetry collection is *What Girls do the Dark* (Nine Arches

Press), and latest novel *The Night Brother* was described by The Times as "a delight...with shades of Angela Carter." In 2019, Val McDermid named her one of the UK's most compelling LGBT writers. www.rosiegarland.com

W.N. Herbert is the author of numerous books of poetry, mostly published by Bloodaxe Books, who brought out his latest collection, *The Wreck of the Fathership,* in 2020. His most recent volume of translations is *The Kindly Interrogator*, translated from the Farsi with the author, Alireza Abiz (Shearsman, 2021). His work has been shortlisted for the T.S.Eliot and Forward Prizes, and has won numerous Arts Council awards. He is the recipient of a Cholmondeley Award, and a Fellow of the Royal Society of Literature. He teaches poetry at Newcastle University, and was until recently Dundee's first Makar.

Ian Humphreys's debut collection *Zebra* (Nine Arches Press, 2019) was nominated for the Portico Prize. He is the editor of *Why I Write Poetry* (Nine Arches Press, 2021) and the producer/ co-editor of a forthcoming anthology on Sylvia Plath (Nine Arches Press, 2022). His work has been highly commended in the Forward Prizes for Poetry and won first prize in the Hamish Canham Prize. A fellow of The Complete Works, Ian's poems are showcased in *Ten: Poets of the New Generation* (Bloodaxe).

Keith Jarrett is a writer, performer and academic. A multiple poetry slam champion, Keith was selected for the International Literary Showcase as one of 10 outstanding LGBT writers in the UK. His poem, 'From the Log Book', was projected onto the façade of St. Paul's Cathedral and broadcast as a commemorative installation. His play, *Safest Spot in Town,* was performed at the Old Vic and aired on BBC Four. *Selah,* his poetry collection, was published in 2017.

Zaffar Kunial was born in Birmingham and lives in Hebden Bridge. His first book – *Us* – was published by Faber & Faber (2018) and shortlisted for awards including the Costa Poetry Award and the T. S. Eliot Prize. Sinead Morrissey says: 'his is a wondrous poetic of loopholes, portals and translations, and of the magic in-between'. A pamphlet, *Six,* was out from Faber in 2019.

Andrew McMillan's first collection, *physical*, was the first poetry collection to win the Guardian First Book Award; it also won a Somerset Maugham Award, an Eric Gregory Award, a Northern Writers' Award and the Aldeburgh First Collection Prize. In 2019 it was voted as one of the top 25 poetry books of the past 25 years by the Booksellers Association. His second collection, *playtime*, won the inaugural Polari Prize. He is a senior lecturer at the Manchester Writing School at Manchester Metropolitan University and is a fellow of the Royal Society of Literature. His third collection is *pandemonium*.

Rachel Mann is a poet, priest, scholar and broadcaster. She is the author of twelve books, including the critically acclaimed poetry collection 'A Kingdom of Love' (Carcanet, 2019). She is a Visiting Teaching Fellow at the Manchester Writing School and a Visiting Scholar at Sarum College. www.rachelmann.co.uk

Kim Moore's first collection *The Art of Falling* was published by Seren in 2015 and won the Geoffrey Faber Memorial Prize. Her second collection *All The Men I Never Married* is forthcoming with Seren in 2021. She has recently completed her doctorate in 'Poetry and Everyday Sexism' at Manchester Metropolitan University and is the co-director of Kendal Poetry Festival.

Pascale Petit was born in Paris, grew up in France and Wales and lives in Cornwall. She is of French/Welsh/Indian heritage. Her eighth collection, *Tiger Girl* (Bloodaxe Books, 2020), was shortlisted for the Forward Prize for Best Collection, won an RSL Literature Matters award while in progress, and a poem from the book won the Keats-Shelley Prize. Her seventh collection, *Mama Amazonica* (Bloodaxe Books, 2017), won the inaugural Laurel Prize, and the RSL's Ondaatje Prize. Four previous collections were shortlisted for the T.S. Eliot Prize.

Jacqueline Saphra is a poet, playwright and teacher. Recent collections are *All My Mad Mothers,* shortlisted for the 2017 T.S. Eliot prize and *Dad, Remember You are Dead* (2019), both from Nine Arches Press. *A Bargain with the Light: Poems after Lee Miller* (2017) and *Veritas: Poems after Artemisia (2020)* were published by

Hercules Editions. Her most recent play, *The Noises* was nominated for a Standing Ovation Award. *One Hundred Lockdown Sonnets* was published by Nine Arches Press in 2021.

Clare Shaw has three poetry collections with Bloodaxe - *Straight Ahead*, *Head On* and *Flood*: her fourth collection *Towards a General Theory of Love* was awarded a Northern Writer's Award and will be published by Bloodaxe in 2022. Clare is co-director of the Kendal Poetry Festival; she works as a project lead and tutor with a range of organisations including the Royal Literary Fund. Clare is also a mental health trainer with a particular interest in trauma, creativity and wellbeing.

Daniel Sluman is a 34-year-old poet and disability rights activist. He co-edited the first major UK Disability poetry anthology *Stairs and Whispers: D/deaf and Disabled Poets Write Back* and has appeared widely in UK poetry journals. He has published three collections with Nine Arches Press, his second, *the terrible*, was released in 2015, and his third collection of poetry, *single window* (2021) is shortlisted for the T. S. Eliot Prize 2021. He tweets @danielsluman

Jean Sprackland has published five collections, most recently *Green Noise* (Cape, 2018), whose poems are 'exact and well-made, their lightness of touch often given drive by a fierce vocabulary' (Literary Review). She was the winner of the Costa Poetry Award in 2008 for *Tilt*. She is also the author of two prose books: *These Silent Mansions*, and *Strands*, which won the Portico Prize for Non-Fiction in 2012. Jean is Professor of Creative Writing at Manchester Metropolitan University.

Born and raised in Hong Kong, **Jennifer Wong** is the author of several collections including *Goldfish* (Chameleon Press) and a pamphlet, *Diary of a Miu Miu Salesgirl* (Bitter Melon Poetry 2019). Her latest collection, 回家 *Letters Home* (Nine Arches Press 2020) was named a Wild Card Choice by Poetry Book Society. She has a creative writing PhD from Oxford Brookes University and teaches creative writing at Poetry School and Oxford Brookes. Her work has appeared in *World Literature Today, Oxford Poetry, Magma Poetry, Poetry Review, Poetry London, PN Review* and *Asian Review of Books*.

Acknowledgements and Works Cited

Introduction by Ian Humphreys: James Baldwin, *The Cross of Redemption: Uncollected Writings* (Vintage International, 2010). Audre Lorde, *Sister Outsiders: Essays and Speeches* (Crossing Press, 1984). *Don't Ask Me What I Mean: Poets in Their Own Words* edited by Clare Brown and Don Paterson (Picador, 2012).

Pusikit: On Working as a Poet Whilst Working for a Living by Romalyn Ante: Anaïs Nin, *The Diary of Anaïs Nin 1947-1955.* (Houghton Mifflin Harcourt, 1975). Richard Blanco, *How to Love a Country* (Beacon Press, 2019). Rainer Maria Rilke. *Letters to a Young Poet.* (W. W. Norton & Company. Revised ed. edition, 1993).

Queering the Poem: On Writing One's Intersectional Truths by Mary Jean Chan: 'The Darkling Thrush', Thomas Hardy, *Collected Poems* (Wordsworth Editions; New edition, 1994). Adrienne Rich, 'Dedications', *An Atlas of the Difficult World* (W. W. Norton & Company, 1991). Audre Lorde, 'A Litany for Survival', *The Collected Poems of Audre Lorde* (W. W. Norton & Company, 1978). Chen Chen, 'I Invite My Parents to a Dinner Party', first published in *Poem-a-Day* on April 19, 2018, by the Academy of American Poets.

In Praise of Emptiness: On Writing about Place and Paying Attention by Jean Sprackland: Letter to Anne Stevenson, Jan 1964, from *Elizabeth Bishop, Prose,* ed Schwartz (Chatto & Windus, 2011). Gaston Bachelard, *The Poetics of Space*, translated by Maria Jolas (Beacon Press, 1994). 'The Major Genius of a Minor Art', by Bryan Appleyard, from *The Times,* 23rd August 1984 https://www.carcanet.co.uk/cgi-bin/scribe?s howdoc=1;doctype=interview

What Is thi langwij a thi guhtr Using Us For? On Poetry and Dialect by W. N. Herbert: Adam Boulton and Val McDermid on Sky News, 9th May 2021. Chic Murray: https://www.youtube.com/watch?v=kC7bQgX6kVc. Theresa Muñoz's 2015 thesis 'Alienation in the Work of Tom Leonard' archived at: https://theses.gla.ac.uk/7028/. G. Gregory Smith, *Scottish Literature: Character and Influence* (London: Macmillan, 1919). Liz Berry, 'Oh Sweethearts': https://www.poetryfoundation.org/poetrymagazine/poems/118577/oh-sweethearts. Charles Dickens, *David Copperfield*, Penguin Classics, 1988). W.S. Graham's 'The Beast in the Space' from *Collected Poems* (Faber & Faber, 1979). Hugh MacDiarmid, 'A Theory of Scots Letters' is reprinted in *The Thistle Rises*, ed. Alan Bold (London: Hamish Hamilton, 1984). Tom Leonard "Unrelated Incidents (1)' from *Intimate Voices* (London: Vintage, 1995). Lewis Hyde, *A Primer for Forgetting* (Edinburgh: Canongate, 2019). William Letford's 'This Is It', https://www.scottishpoetrylibrary.org.uk/poem/it-0/

Un Enfoque Latinx: On Writing in Two Languages by Leo Boix: 'Un Enfoque Latinx: On Writing in Two Languages': Ed Morales, *Latinx: The New Force in American Politics and Culture* (Verso, 2018)

Variations: On Writing as a Feminist and Against Sexism by Kim Moore: Sara Ahmed, *Living a Feminist Life* (Duke University Press, 2017). John Berger, *Ways of Seeing* (Penguin, 1972). Audre Lorde, *Sister Outsider: Essays and Speeches* (The Crossing Press, 1984). bell hooks, *Talking Back: Thinking Feminist, Thinking Black* (South End Press, 1989). Virginia Woolf, 'A Sketch of the Past', *Moments of Being* (Harvest Books, 1985). Adrienne Rich, 'Husband-Right and Father-Right'. *On Lies, Secrets and Silence: Selected Prose 1966-1978.* (W. W. Norton & Co., 1977). Luce Irigaray, *To Be Two* (The Athlone Press, 2000). Jonathan Culler, *Theory of the Lyric.* (Harvard University Press, 2015) Carolyn Forché, *Against Forgetting: Twentieth Century Poetry of Witness.* (W. W. Norton & Co., 1993). Mary Jean Chan, 'Towards a poetics of racial trauma: lyric hybridity in Claudia Rankine's Citizen.' (*Journal of American Studies,* 52, 2018).

Don't Fence Me In: On Writing Across Genres by Rosie Garland: Lewis Carroll, *Alice Through the Looking Glass* (Macmillan, 1871). Joan Didion, 'Why I Write' (New York Times, December 5th 1976). F. Scott Fitzgerald, *The Crack-Up* (New Directions, 1945). Rosie Garland, 'Exit Ophelia', in *Escape Wheel* (GWFM New York, 2019). Tove Jansson, Fair Play (Sort of Books, 1989). Audre Lorde, 'Poetry is not a luxury' from *Selected Works,* ed. Roxane Gay (W. W. Norton & Company 2020). Herb Magidson & Carl Sigman, 'Enjoy yourself, it's later than you think' (Decca Records, 1949). Iggy Pop, The John Peel Lecture (BBC Music, 19 October 2014). Cole Porter & Robert Fletcher, 'Don't Fence Me In' (Warner Chappell Music, 1934). Rebecca Solnit, *Hope in the Dark* (Haymarket Books, 2016). Walt Whitman, 'Song of Myself, 51' from *Leaves of Grass,* (1855). Oscar Wilde, *The Picture of Dorian Gray* (Ward, Lock & Co 1891). Virginia Woolf, *Orlando* (Hogarth Press, 1928).

How I Built a New Voice: On Writing and Living as a Disabled Poet by Daniel Sluman: Robert Lowell, *Lord Weary's Castle* (Mariner, 1983). Robert Lowell, *Life Studies* (Faber, 2001). Ted Hughes, *Crow*

(Faber, 2001). Ted Hughes, *Birthday Letters* (Faber, 1999). Charles Olson's Projective Verse: https://www.poetryfoundation.org/articles/69406/projective-verse. Jennifer Bartlett interview about Larry Eigner: https://www.poetryfoundation.org/poetrymagazine/articles/70179/disability-and-poetry. Sarah Juliet Lauro, 'Into the White: Larry Eigner's Meta-physical Poetics': http://dsq-sds.org/article/view/3354/3528

The Long Game: On Making a Life in Poetry by Sarah Corbett: Sarah Corbett, 'The Commute', *A Perfect Mirror* (Pavilion Poetry / Liverpool University Press, 2018). Seamus Heaney, 'Station Island', *Station Island* (Faber & Faber, 1984). Gerard Manly Hopkins, 'God's Grandeur', *Poems and Prose* (Penguin Classics, 1985).

Poetry as Patrìn: On Writing Your Truth, Not Someone Else's by Jo Clement: Simon Kövesi, 'Interview with David Morley: The Gypsy and the Poet', *John Clare Society Journal*, 32 (2013), 51. David MacRitchie, 'Scottish Gypsies Under the Stewarts', *Journal of the Gypsy Lore Society*, 1 (1890-91), 335. Robert Pinsky, *Gulf Music* (Farrar, Straus & Giroux, 2007). Don Paterson, *The Poem: Lyric, Sign, Metre* (Faber, 2018). W. N. Herbert, *Writing Poetry* (Routledge, 2010). Mary Oliver, *A Poetry Handbook* (Harvest, 1994). Peter Sansom, *Writing Poems* (Bloodaxe, 1994). Sergei Shubin and Kate Swanson, '"I'm an imaginary figure": Unravelling the mobility and marginalisation of Scottish Gypsy Travellers', Geoforum, 41/6 (November 2010). Kalwant Bhopal, 'Gypsy Travellers and Education: Changing Needs and Changing Perceptions', *British Journal of Educational Studies* (2004). Maria Rainer Rilke, trans. David Cook, *The Sonnets to Orpheus* (Redcliffe Press, 2012).

Keep Ithaka Always in Your Mind: On the Journey and the Value of Poetry by Jacqueline Saphra: CP Cavafy, 'Ithaka', translated by Edmund Keeley and Philip Sherrard, from *C.P. Cavafy: Collected Poems* (Princeton University Press, 1975). William Carlos Williams, *Asphodel, that Greeny Flower & Other Love Poems* (New Editions, 1994). William Ernest Henley, 'Invictus' from *The Oxford Book of English Verse*, ed. Arthur Quiller Couch (1900). Anna Akhmatova, 'Requiem', translated by Alex Cigale (*Hopkins Review*, archived at: https://hopkinsreview.jhu.edu/archive/requiem/).

Poem-making as Anticolonial Assemblage: On the Decolonisation of Poetry by Khairani Barokka: Eve Tuck and K. Wayne Yang, from 'Decolonization is not a metaphor', *Decolonization: Indigeneity, education & society*, 1(1) 2012.

Poetry Saved My Life: On Writing About Trauma by Clare Shaw: Maya Angelou, *I Know Why the Caged Bird Sings* (Random House, 1969). Kei Miller, *A Light Song of Light* (Carcanet, 2010). Karen A. Baikie and Kay Wilhelm, 'Emotional and physical health benefits of expressive writing', *Advances in Psychiatric Treatment*, (September 2005), 338–46. (Published online, Cambridge University Press, 2 January 2018). Susan J. Brison, *Aftermath: Violence and the Remaking of a Self* (Princeton, 2002). Erin Vincent, 'They say writing is cathartic, but writing about my parents dying almost killed me', *The Guardian* (11 April 2017). Muriel Rukeyser, 'The Speed of Darkness', in *The Speed of Darkness* (Random House, 1968). Tadeusz Różewicz, 'In the Middle of Life' (1956), in *Sobbing Superpower: Selected Poems of Tadeusz Różewicz* (Norton, 2011). Gregory Orr, *Poetry As Survival* (University of Georgia Press, 2002). Claire Shaw: *Towards a General Theory of Love* (Bloodaxe, 2022), *Straight Ahead* (Bloodaxe, 2006), *Flood* (Bloodaxe, 2018), and *Head On* (Bloodaxe, 2012). Claire Shaw: 'My Story, My Words: A Practical Guide to Creative Writing for Survivors of Sexual Abuse and Violence' (2021) http://clearlines.org.uk/wp-content/uploads/2021/05/Clear-Lines-Creative-Writing-Guide-for-Survivors.pdf. Kim Moore, 'When I Open', *The North,* 58 (Summer 2017). Katrina Naomi, 'Responding to Violence', *Magma,* 62 (2015). Bertolt Brecht, 'Motto' (1939), in *Bertolt Brecht: Poems 1913-1956,* eds. John Willett and Ralph Manhaim (Eyre Methuen, 1976).

Become a Different Bird: On Changing Your Poetry (And Maybe Also You) by Rishi Dastidar: Durs Grünbein, 'Biological Waltz', *POETRY*, October 1998, (https://www.poetryfoundation.org/poetrymagazine/browse?contentId=40356); see also (trans Michael Hofmann), *Ashes for Breakfast: Selected Poems* (Faber & Faber, 2006). Robert Herrick, 'To Daffodils' (https://www.poetryfoundation.org/poems/47335/to-daffodils); see also, *Poems* selected by Stephen Romer (Faber & Faber, 2010). John McCullough, 'Soulcraft', from *Reckless Paper Birds* (Penned in the Margins, 2019). Edna St Vincent Millay, 'I will put Chaos into fourteen lines', from *Mine the Harvest* (Harper and Brothers, 1954); http://bactra.org/Poetry/Millay/I_will_put_Chaos_into_fourteen_lines.html Mary Ruefle, *Madness, Rack, and Honey: Collected Lectures* (Wave Books, 2012).

The World's Strongest Men: On Writing About Family by Jonathan Edwards: 'Gregory Peck and Sophia Loren in Crumlin for the Filming of *Arabesque,* June 1965', from *My Family and Other Superheroes* (Seren, 2014) 'My Father Buying Sweets', 1956 from *Gen* (Seren, 2018).